• *Mystic Celia* •

Mystic Celia

Order this book online at www.trafford.com/07-1259
or email orders@trafford.com

Most Trafford titles are also available at major online book retailers.

Set in Galliard • Cover and interior designed by Robin Locke Monda
Cover illustrated by Layi Babatunde
Author photograph by M. Nelson

Note for Librarians: A cataloguing record for this book is available from Library and Archives Canada at www.collectionscanada.ca/amicus/index-e.html

ISBN: 978-1-4251-2409-0

We at Trafford believe that it is the responsibility of us all, as both individuals and corporations, to make choices that are environmentally and socially sound. You, in turn, are supporting this responsible conduct each time you purchase a Trafford book, or make use of our publishing services. To find out how you are helping, please visit www.trafford.com/responsiblepublishing.html

Our mission is to efficiently provide the world's finest, most comprehensive book publishing service, enabling every author to experience success. To find out how to publish your book, your way, and have it available worldwide, visit us online at www.trafford.com/10510

www.trafford.com

North America & international
toll-free: 1 888 232 4444 (USA & Canada)
phone: 250 383 6864 • fax: 250 383 6804
email: info@trafford.com

The United Kingdom & Europe
phone: +44 (0)1865 722 113 • local rate: 0845 230 9601
facsimile: +44 (0)1865 722 868 • email: info.uk@trafford.com

10 9 8 7 6 5 4 3 2

Mystic Celia

A MEMOIR

Layi Babatunde

"Fever," Peggy Lee

A Journal of Love

I am Layi Babatunde. I am a Nigerian prince from the place of Oyo. I carry the spirit of my grandfather. I am caretaker of my father's wife. I am a beacon in our Dark Community and I light the way for my sister's children. I walk with the pride of humankind. This is my charge. It is my destiny, yet my ore—my gift of God. But, I call for my goddess. I need her strength and her beauty to highlight the essence of life itself. I feel her presence ever with me, but not close enough to touch. I seek her universally in heart, mind and spirit. I thirst for the elusive, mystical, Celia.

I have many things to do and people to love. But, I do not have enough time left to do these. Therefore, I am taking charge of tomorrow; today and tomorrow are still yet to come. When tomorrow finally comes, will I still be here?

Century is very contemptuous. It is mid-Thursday.
Be careful of how you use it. You cannot use it on Wednesday.

To my great mentor and cousin,
Ajibade Oluokum

In memory of Frederick Ibikunle George

Dedication

To my late father and mother of Akin-Ajonbadi Compound of Oyo in Oyo State of Nigeria: great mother Alice Agbeke George, great uncle Olatunji Kufeji, great aunt Titilola Abebi Cole, all of whom I love very dearly. All of to whom my emotional and spiritual being is attached for eternity. May your souls rest in everlasting peace, cradled in the great arms of our Creator.

Acknowledgements

I owe a debt of gratitude to the University of Hawaii Ground and Physical Plan Safety staff, for saving my life when I nearly drowned on June 14, 1969, and to the University for giving me a wonderful education.

I am also grateful to David Bess, Dean of the College of Business Administration and the late Professor Joe Keeler of the Department of Agricultural Economics, for their excellent advice and guidance throughout the course of my studies.

I would like to thank June Naughton of the International Student's Office, as well as Ted and Nancy Fritzchel of the Lutheran Church whose friendship contributed immensely to my emotional well being and happiness in Hawaii.

I would also like to thank the following for their love and friendship: Leo and Patricia Nelson and their family, Janet Evans of Houston, Dr. Jonathan and Carol Braide, Darius Jonathan, Dr. Harrison Mekako, Michael Ashman, Victor Askman, Leo Robinson and Yvonne Hazlewood.

Finally, I would like to give special thanks to Lisa Kaye Babbage Jackson, with whom I share a long and treasured friendship.

Introduction

It seems like yesterday, I was young and vibrant. I had no clue of what the world had for me. But, I had a dream and running ambition to travel and see the world. My subconscious mind traveled around the world to see wonderful and beautiful places. Returning to my conscious mind, it was like Sir Arthur Lewis Economic Theory "Bright Light." I wanted to be part of it. I struggled with my dream wondering if my dream will ever be fulfilled. It was my secret ambition that I had never revealed to anyone, not to any member of my family and not to my friends in our neighborhood. However, I had advantages. I was well placed and privileged. I grew up in a loving Christian family. Our Patriarch, Frederick Ibikunle George, M.B.E.J.P., Member of British Empire and Justice of Peace. He was the first black town warden and he was part of the permanent establishment in British colonial rule. He was in charge of highways, bridges and street layout. He was one of the most important people in Lagos City and also in our Methodist church.

F.I. George, as British establishment popularly knew him, was a motivator and disciplinarian with deep Christian values. Our Matriarch was a homemaker with deep family values. We were raised in a wonderful family setting and outstanding in our neighborhood. The neighborhood was approximately two square miles and the street where we lived ran from east to west off Lagoon, the river that surrounded Lagos Island. In our neighborhood there were many churches as well as mosques. Despite differences in religious beliefs, the Christians and Muslims treated one another like brothers and sisters. It was like a Utopian society, but it was real. In the whole neighborhood, no one ever locked their doors. There were no police parading our streets. There was no need for that. No crimes were ever committed. We had boys and girls clubs and we organized various social activities. Everything was copasetic in the neighborhood. There was no hospital. The British government provided none. We had one doctor for fifty thousand people, a 65 year-old doctor named Labinjo, who was trained and practiced medicine in Scotland for many years before he later returned to the neighborhood to establish a clinic. He performed various medical functions: general medicine, surgery and obstetrics. He also was involved in social organizations in the neighborhood. Everybody seemed to be socially, physically and mentally healthy. However, it was the ambition of every child in the neighborhood to seek higher education in Britain and prepare ourselves to take over the leadership of our country after the departure of British colonial rule, which we believed would inevitably come. However, many people dream but they never do much about it. They sit around and keep dreaming. But I am not that type. I dream and I always work hard to fulfill my ambition and make my dreams come true.

CHAPTER I

London Experience

Monday, August 28 was just another normal day in my home and in the neighborhood. The time had come for me to pursue my ambition to leave my beloved country and my loving family who raised me from childhood and begin my journey to the western world. Departing from my values, everything I grew up with and knew was very painful, but this had always been my dream and my ambition to see the world. At nightfall, on August 28, I boarded Air France to begin my journey to the west.

Eight hours later, from Lagos to Paris, our plane touched down in the Paris airport. It was my first time ever aboard an airplane but the flight was magical, smooth and beautiful. The plane parked a short distance, about two hundred yards from the terminal. I realized that I was in a different world. Everything was different. The people and the environment were different from where I came from, white and very modern. I began to wonder why the British had failed to provide us with this wonderful life. I was very impressed and at the same time angry with British neglects. Although I was very impressed, Paris was not my destination. We had a brief stop, about one hour. I walked around and I made an attempt to speak English to a French boy about my age who happened to be walking near me. He looked at me and then I was coldly ignored. I was shocked and quickly retreated to my shell. But, I was not worried or intimidated; I knew that I was just passing through. My destination was London, England. The United Kingdom was where I intended to be and achieve my goal. After a one hour stopover in Paris, we boarded another flight for London. Exactly one hour later, I finally arrived at my destination, London. It was about eleven o'clock in the morning when the plane touched down at Heathrow, London's airport. After going through an emigration procedure, I had to walk to the luggage claim and I knew that my sister, who had been living in London for the past two years, would be at the airport to welcome me.

As I walked out of the terminal, the first black person I saw was my sister. It was a very happy reunion. I was very happy to see her. However, at first sight of London, I was very disappointed and I did no like London. I did not like the unwelcome attitudes of Londoners. I was very frightened back home because the colonial government brainwashed us to believe that Nigerian citizens have the status of British and commonwealth citizenship. On my arrival in London, I found that to be false. The English does not welcome colored people, as they call us, with open arms to their midst. They were very cold and prejudiced. However, I was very impressed with British orderliness, the quality of life and the availability of basic necessities to Londoners and Colored People. London good life helped me to get adjusted in a very short time.

My sister and I took a crowded tube, the underground train, to Victoria Station in the city. The tube was frightening to me because I had never been on such a gigantic train. There wee boys and girls of my age holding hands and kissing on the train. It was a cultural shock. Back home, boys and girls walk on demarcation lines, no touching and no kissing. Public displays of affection are strictly forbidden. London roads were very organized, clean and narrow. There were many automobiles, red double-decker buses and many black taxis. The worst of all for me was that it was too cold. It was the end of August and the weather was freezing. Everything about London seemed repulsive. I was very disappointed. It was like a boulevard of broken dreams. This is a different world from the one I came from. I became homesick. I missed my home "89." I missed my loving family and my beloved country. "89" is a memorable number. It is the number of our family home. 89 Apongbon Street, in the city of Lagos, situated in our peaceful neighborhood. I missed everything about home.

Two weeks after my arrival, I became well adjusted and became a Londoner. The feeling of homesickness and disappointment with London disappeared. In London, you are in the crowd but you are lonely as hell. People are as cold as the minus zero weather in the month of January. I had been living in London for five months. The first words ever spoken to me by an English person at the bus stop were "Cold, isn't it?" What a stupid question. Of course, it was cold! It was twenty degrees below zero. I took a look at him and responded, "I don't have to answer that question." Here, I was expressing my anger and frustration.

Perhaps the most difficult and worst time of my life was my first winter in London. In the first six months, I did not do much of anything. I was taking my time. I did not rush. I really wanted to get accustomed to London. I really wanted to get accustomed to London's weather and environment before starting on my goal and dreams. However, no matter how cold and uncomfortable the weather was for me, I managed to get a job and put money in my pocket for food and to pay my rent. I found British people at the time to be equal opportunity employers. Within six weeks of my arrival in London, I set out to look for a job. I held the bull by the horns. I was very blunt and very aggressive. I went to one of the hotels in the city of London and walked straight to the personnel office and requested that I be given a job. The personnel manager looked at me and seemed very surprised. However, his response was, "What are you qualified to do? Do you have experience?"

I had no experience. I had not worked in a hotel before. But, I knew how to sweep the floor. I could wash the toilet, and I could wash dishes. That was my experience. We were trained at home to sweep, wash and live in a clean environment. If you employ me, I will work hard to keep your hotel clean. I made it clear to the manager that I was only requesting to be a janitor.

"All right lad," as he called me. I looked around and there was nobody in his office but the two of us, him and me.
"Who is he talking to? Is he responding to my request or is he talking to somebody else, but my name is not Lad?" I thought.
Anyway, it was close enough. "Are you talking to me?" I inquired.

"Yes, of course, I am talking to you. Are you really looking for a job or do you want something to eat?"

"Sir, I am looking for a job."

"The pay is $21.00 dollars a week, free breakfast and lunch; eight hours, 7 a.m. to 4 p.m.; one hour break and you are required to work on weekends. Now, when can you start?"
I took a look at my watch. It was 8:45 a.m. "Well," I said, "I can start today. I mean now!" He seemed surprised at my enthusiasm for a janitorial job.

He asked his secretary to take me to the tearoom and wait there.

The secretary was an English girl about eighteen years old and very attractive. She gave me a cup of tea and asked me to wait for the manager. I was very impressed. I couldn't believe that English people could be personable and friendly. Yes, I am going to enjoy working here. After half an hour of waiting and drinking tea, the manager came to me and said, "All right Lad, follow me, I am taking you to the locker room." When we arrived at the locker room, he issued me a locker, two sets of clean uniforms and two sets of aprons. He asked me to change and come back to his office. I was very enthusiastic about the job. I needed money to prepare myself and pursue my ambition and to make my dreams become reality. I returned to the manager's office.

When I got there, a young Irish gentleman was waiting for me. He quickly introduced himself to me, "My name is John O'Reilly. Follow me. I am the supervisor at the dish room." I had no clue what I was getting myself into.

New Cavendish is a five star hotel located in the heart of London. It is one of the biggest hotels in London with a huge dining room, big enough to sit thousands of people. It also has a restaurant attached to it. All dirty dishes from the dining room and restaurant come to the dish room to be washed. It was already eleven o'clock in the morning and all these dishes must be washed and ready for lunch at twelve o'clock. With only one hour to go, there was no time to waste. For one minute, I stood there looking at the dishes, piled up like mountains. I became scared. However, there was no going back. I must work and I needed that job. John, my supervisor, was a very nice man. He worked with many Africans in the past. He understood our problems. We need the job and we want to work but are not accustomed to this type of work.

Generally, Irish people in London were very understanding and personable to the black people. Carefully, John introduced me to the operations. There was a conveyor belt stretch piled high as a mountain waiting for me in the operations. There are chemicals to apply and you must know the application quantity and when to apply. More importantly, you must be fast to meet the speed of the machine. My first day on the job was hell. I did my best because I did not want to disappoint John. My supervisor noticed that my performance on the job was below standard but was willing to give me more time. After I was on the job for eight days, my performance on the job was still below the standard. John had to let me go and I was dismissed. I collected my pay $21.00 minus taxes. The net pay carried me to my next job.

On the following Monday, I set out at 9 a.m. to look for another job. As I was going from door to door in the business district or any place or building that looked like a business. I saw a fairly large building. It looked like a hospital. I saw ambulances going in and out of the building. I walked around the building then I saw the sign "HELP WANTED." I walked right in to apply.

"Good morning."

"Good morning lad."

"I come to apply for a job."

"Okay lad, fill this form out for me."

I filled out the form and returned it to him.

"Are you ready for work?" This was a funeral home. "Here, we prepare the dead for burial. Your job is washing and cleaning up the dead. This is a piece of work. Each body pays you and your pay is five pounds per wash. On a busy day, you may wash three to five bodies and you can come any day you choose. Are you ready for work?"

Three to five bodies at five pounds is $15.00 t $25.00 a day. Yes, I was ready to work.

The manager took me to the washing area. There were two English boys there. They responded very coldly. It was clear that they didn't like me. The manager went on to show me the procedure. The body was placed on a conveyor belt from the other end, covered with a white sheet and when the light is on, you pressed the button to bring the body to you to be washed.

The first day, I washed two bodies and received ten pounds ($30). This was a lot of money to me. The second day when I showed up for work only Jim came to work. Ted did not come. Five minutes later, Jim also disappeared. I was the only one at the wash. I was happy. I thought to myself, "It is going to be a busy day and I will make money."

A half-hour later, there was a green light on the line indicating that there was a dead body on the conveyor belt to be washed. I pressed the button to bring the body to the washing point. The body came and I pressed the red button to stop and turned on the water to start washing what appeared to be a dead body, but to my astonishment, it jumped up and gave me a hard slap on my face. Needless to say, it was very scary.

I thought, "I didn't know this person and didn't have anything to do with its death. I ran out of the building. When I got home, I called the manager and I told him what had happened and told him that I would not be coming back and I wanted him to mail me my check. The manager laughed, and told me that my co-workers, the two English boys, Jim and Ted were playing a prank on me, but I refused to return to the job.

The following day, I started out to seek another job. Fortunately, I didn't have to go far. I took the tube from Clapham Common station, one stop to Clapham North. I decided to get out of the train and start searching for a job. I went from office to office and door to door in the business district. I walked only one block to a building, No. 84 The Chase Clapham, which was a film, camera and cinema projector warehouse.

I went into the building and very directly, "Good morning", I said.

"Good morning, lad, may I help you?"

"Yes, I am looking for a job."

"What type of job are you looking for?"

"Any job that is available, but, I can work for an account office as an account clerk."

"You need to talk with our personnel manager."

"Please come in lad. What can I do for you?"

"I came to apply for a job as an account clerk."

"How did you know about our company?"

"I was walking around to look for a job and decided to approach this company. Please, do you have any jobs available?"

"Yes, the only job we have available is shipping clerk."

"Thank you sir, very good, I will take it. I once worked for a British company (John Holt) in the shipping department.

But, it was not in England. it was in Nigeria." I was lying.

"That is very good. We have one Nigerian working here in the shipping department. His name is Tom. Do you know him?"

"I may know him. I'm not sure. Can I meet him?"

The personnel manager picked up the telephone and called the shipping supervisor. "Jim, please send Tom to my office."

To my surprise, Fatai Kamoju, one of my neighborhood friends I left behind was already here. "Yes, I know Tom, we were childhood friends."

"Very good, I hope the both of you will be happy with us. Fill out the employment form and I will call the supervisor to introduce you to the rest of the staff. ""Thank God!" I exclaimed. I got the job, but wait a minute: "How much is the pay?"

After I completed the employment form, the personnel manager reviewed it and said, very good, and he went on to explain the nature of the job. "You will be employed as a shipping clerk. You will be working in the warehouse with Tom. The nature of your job is receiving, packing and shipping. The hours are from 8 a.m. to 5 p.m., with one hour for lunch, Monday through Friday, 40 hours a week. We also have two fifteen minute tea breaks at 10 o'clock and at 3 o'clock daily. The salary is eight pounds and ten shillings ($31) a week. Well lad, when can you start?"

I took a look at my wristwatch, it was 8:30 a.m. and said, "May I start now sir?" The manager picked up the telephone and called the warehouse supervisor, Jim.

"Please follow me," said Jim. "I am your supervisor. I hope you will be happy here with us."

"Thank you, sir." I got the job and the work began.

The job was very hard and physically demanding. It was mostly loading and offloading the trailer. It also involved packing and lifting heavy boxes, which I was not physically and mentally prepared for. However, no matter what the obstacles, I was determined to stay on the job. The first three days on the job were very difficult. Every muscle in my body was aching. I depended on aspirin and painkillers to engage me to sleep.

After three days of working, my performance was better than average. I became fully employed and every Friday, six pounds and sixteen shillings (about $27.00 net) kept coming and that was just enough for me. I ate very well and my rent was fully paid. I was staying in a small room, an attic over 27 Gibson Square, Islington, North London. The rent was one pound and ten shillings (about $7 per week). I had money for transportation and to go to the movies occasionally. However, I was not socially active because I was preoccupied with my many ambitions. I had wanted to follow the footsteps of our family Patriarch, Mr. F.I. George. I wanted to be an architect, a civil engineer and an urban planner. My goal was to return home and become a city engineer, warden or possibly the mayor.

However, working in a film, cinema projector warehouse changed my goals. I became interested in photography and cinematography. Motion pictures became my utmost interest with the hope of returning home and making documentary pictures for the country or perhaps becoming director of the National Broadcasting Corporation. My imagination and ambition were running wild. After being on the job for four weeks, I had managed to put some money in the bank. I decided to take a course in cinema, so I enrolled in the British Film Institute to study cinema. However, after six months, I dropped out of the institute. I started spending more time at U.S.I.S. (The United States Information Services) in London where I read a great deal of books on film, cinema and photography and hit upon the idea of studying in the United States of America.

After eleven months on the job, everything seemed to be going well for me, so I thought I must take a one-week holiday to visit my childhood friend, H.O. Adeosun, who was studying electrical engineering in Manchester City, and to have some time searching for a good school of photography in the United States. The first school I came across was New York Institute of Photography which advertised and was well represented in the New Yorker magazine. I quickly sent my application for admission.

Then I left for Manchester City to visit my friend. In September, early one Saturday morning, I boarded a luxury coach from King Cross St. Pancreas, London for a six-hour journey to Manchester City. The coach arrived early in the afternoon. My friend was at the station to meet me and we went straight to the football stadium to watch the game between Manchester City and Nottingham City. My weekend in Manchester City was a very wonderful experience. Sunday afternoon my friend, H.A. Andeosun, took me on a bus tour of the center of the city. As I was riding on the bus a strange feeling came over me. I began to feel as though I once lived here. I recalled perfectly that I was once part of this city. As the bus drove around the city, I became convinced that I once existed in this city. Could it be that I was an English person in my past life? When we returned home late that night, the thought of having lived a past life was very much on my mind throughout the night until I fell asleep and the mystery began.

CHAPTER II

Manchester City

Betty Bethards asked, what is a dream? Are dreams some strange mysterious phenomenon that spontaneously happen on the night shift of life? Or, is there some deeper meaning behind the universal experience?

The mystery of being in Manchester City in the past was overwhelmingly on my mind at bedtime. I could not sleep. I was tossing and turning. But gradually, I fell asleep. But, it was not a restful sleep. It was a journey back to the past life. As I suddenly fell asleep and was deep in a dream, I was lying on a bed next to a young, slim, beautiful English woman holding a Bible in her hands and two English doctors dressed in white laboratory gowns. The two doctors were each standing on opposite sides of the bed performing surgery on me, my eyeballs were removed from my eye sockets and I was left with two six inch holes in my head. When I woke up in the morning, I was very relieved that the six-hour ordeal was just a dream.

However, my first Monday in Manchester City was a brand new day. My host had left for work and I was home alone with much of nothing to do. I decided to take a trip to the park in downtown Manchester City.

It was the middle of September; the weather was not yet cold but very chilly and windy. The sun was shining brightly over the park. The trees and flowers were neatly planted and beautifully manicured. There were clean and comfortable chairs and benches for everyone in the park to relax. I was very impressed. I decided to spend my afternoon there. Soon, I was on the bench enjoying the beautiful environment and hoping to be alone with a wonderful environment created by man.

Ten minutes of sitting and wondering, a young woman with

ravishing beauty walked straight into my life. She appeared to be the same person from my six hour dream of last night. "Oh God," I said trembling with fear. This is déjà vu all over again. I thought I was back in the dream.

The first words she spoke to me were, "Chilly and windy, isn't it?"

"Yes, it is," I answered.

She went on: "Hello, my name is Celia, and what is your name?"

"My name is Emanuel, but you can call me Layi."

Celia: "I LIKE Layi. I will call you Layi. It is a beautiful, unusual name."

Layi: "Thank you."

Celia: "If you will excuse me, give me a moment, I will be right back. Could you wait for me?"

Layi: "I will wait for you Celia."

Celia: "Layi, I would like you to meet my daughter."

She opened the baby carriage. I was swept off my feet. She was the most beautiful bi-racial baby I had ever seen. Her skin was chocolate brown. Her face was very smooth. She had light brown eyes and her hair was like silk. Her nose and mouth were specially shaped; she was a baby angel.

"This baby is a special God's creation," I said to myself. I fell in love right away with the mother and her baby. I had a desire to take them to London with me and take care of them.

Layi: "She is very beautiful."

Celia: "Thank you. Layi, what do you do? Do you live in Manchester City?"

Layi: "No, I came from London. I am visiting a friend here in

Manchester City. What about you? What do you do?"

Celia: "Right now, I am a full-time mother. I am taking care of my daughter. What about you. What do you do? What are you doing in London?"

Layi: "I work in a camera warehouse as a shipping clerk."

Celia: "Do you like Manchester City?"

Layi: "Yes, I like this quiet beautiful environment. I have a strong feeling I once lived here."

Celia: "Could it be that you lived, died and now live again? Are you a British person?"

Layi: "No, I am African. I came to London from Nigeria about one year ago."

Celia: "Nigeria? I once lived in Nigeria. My father worked in a church there. We returned to Manchester City when I was very young."

Layi: "You and I have something in common. We have traveled to other places. Traveling is my passion. I am very sure it is yours too. Besides living in Nigeria, have you traveled outside of Manchester City since you have returned?"

Celia: "Physical realm? No. But, I had traveled and communicated with the whole world in spirit. I am special. You can only find me in unusual places, or you will never find me at all. I am like a river. I flow in one direction and constantly move. It is difficult to meet me twice in one place. I communicate only with the subconscious mind. Right now, I am communicating with your subconscious mind. However, if you are my man, I mean, if you and I are on the same spiritual frequency, I can go anywhere to be with you for a very long time."

Layi: "Celia, I love you and I want to be with you. Can I be with you?"

Celia: "Layi, it is not easy to love me and be in my company, you have to earn it."

Layi: "What would I do to earn your love?"

Celia: "Layi, my love is very precious. Two things you must do. You must give me your subconscious mind, and second, you must obey my command. But do not worry, I already have your subconscious mind and I am very sure you will obey my orders. Layi, you are my man. By the way, I knew you were going to be here and that is why I came with my daughter to meet you."

Layi: "Thank you, Celia. May I hold her?"

As Celia lifted her daughter from the seat, I saw a white bible. It was the same Bible carried by the lady that I saw with the two English doctors who performed surgery on my eyes in my dream the night before. It was very amazing. Celia handed her daughter to me. She was a very beautiful baby. I was overwhelmed. I became deeply in love with the baby and the mother.

Layi: "Celia, who is the father?"

Celia: "She is my daughter and that is all you need to know. You must not worry about details."

Layi: "Would you and your daughter come to London with me?"

Celia: "You are very adorable Layi, but what about your dreams, your ambitions and aspirations?"

Layi: "Don't worry. You and your daughter are now a part of my dreams."

Celia: "Layi, I want you to understand perfectly. I am here with you today. It does not mean that you will see me again tomorrow. Remember, I am like a river. I flow continuously. You will not see me twice in one place, unless we were on the same frequency. Layi, my daughter and I love you very much. You are my man and we will always be with you. We will come to London but you will not see us physically. You will only feel our presence. We will control your dreams and social life. Please understand, we were part of your past life. The two things you must do when you return to London, you must go to the United States Embassy to seek a traveling visa. I know very well that you have ambitions to travel around the world. I have now entered your dreams and every step you take will be controlled by me.

For six hours, I had been subconsciously listening to Celia. I fell deeply in love with her and her daughter. I did not want to leave her in the park but the sun had disappeared from the sky. It was getting very dark and my host must have returned home from work and he must be wondering where I am.

I spent four days in Manchester City. However, I did not go back to the park to look for Celia and her daughter. I returned to London on Sunday night to get ready for work on Monday morning. On Monday morning, when I woke up, I felt a burning in my left eye. The burning became so intense that I was forced to see a neighborhood doctor who gave me an eye checkup and quickly referred me to the Moorefield Eye Hospital in North London. When I arrived at the hospital, I met a nurse and two English doctors who closely resembled the doctors who performed surgery on my eyes in my dream the night before I met Celia in the park. These two doctors gave me a thorough and extensive eye exam and they decided that I needed surgery on my left eye. After the successful surgery, I was wheeled to the recovery room and I fell into my subconscious mind. Then Celia reappeared. She came to my bedside with six red roses.

Attached was a beautiful note. "Get well and be ready for our journey." After three days in the hospital, I was well recuperated and was discharged from the hospital. When I got back to my room, I found a reply from my application for admission to the New York Institute of Photography had arrived. I was accepted.

Then, I remembered what Celia once said to me through my subconscious mind: "Layi, be ready, you and I are going to take a mysterious journey. In October or the middle of November, I will meet you in Southampton where our journey will start. I will meet you at the library aboard a luxury ship, her Majesty Queen Elizabeth II. We will be together for ten hours from Southampton, England to Cherbourg, France. Then, I will leave you to continue the journey alone. You will be lonely and miserable for five days until you arrive in New York City. But do not worry. I will meet you again in New York City. You will see me again at a party at the International House on Riverside Drive in New York City.

"I will be at the party but you will not recognize me. I will wait to have a last dance with you to a beautiful song by Peggy Lee, 'Fever.' Then I will leave. Layi, listen, our next meeting will be in California. These are the things you must know and do.

"Pick up a magazine and check the pen pal section. My name is in the book. My name will be Wilma Browne and my address is 16 Warring Street, Seaside, California. Write me a letter. I will become your pen pal and from there I will meet you and we will have sex for the first time.

"Now, these are the things you must remember. You must remember Eight Oxford Street, definitely. You will experience ecstasy when I lay in bed next to you there. And, many months later our daughter will join us. But don't get excited. You will probably not be in control of the whole affair.

"Seventeen years later, in the month of September, you will know about our daughter. Around June 1987, our daughter will start searching for her father. She will take a trip to the campus of the University of Hawaii in Honolulu, but she will miss you. In September, when you come to the campus, she would have left Honolulu and returned to Los Angeles.

"You never meet our daughter but consciously and subconsciously, you love your daughter very dearly. Remember, your college mate will inform you that you have a daughter on the campus. You will initiate a strong search for her, but it would have been too late. It will be a long rough road to find her but don't worry, you will get some help along the way. To find your daughter, it is necessary to remember the years you spent in Los Angeles, California in 1968 and 1969. More importantly, you must remember Carol Cunningham, Evelyn and Elaine Gima and the Y.W.C.A. Hotel, Los Angeles, California."

CHAPTER III

Back to London

It was a mystery. After fully recovering from my eye surgery I was discharged from the hospital and returned to my house. Celia's orders and instructions in my subconscious mind began to emerge. My application for admission to the New York Institute of Photography arrived and it was approved. When I returned to work, after my surgery, I took the letter with me and during lunchtime, went to the United States Embassy to apply for a student visa. Fortunately and unexpectedly, my application was approved. I began to wonder if Celia Parson's spiritual power had something to do with these series of events. However, my major problem remained. I had little or no money to finance my education and to travel to the United States within 52 days, after which my student visa would be expired. It was the first week of October and my visa expired on November 22. I checked with my bank account. I had only two hundred pounds in my account. After paying my fare to the United States, I would be left with very little for my education and living expenses.

I appealed to my sister in London and my best friend in Manchester City for a loan. Fortunately, I received a loan of fifty pounds from each of them; not enough to pay my fare to the United States. In addition to the loan of fifty, another friend suggested that I give up my room so that I could save the money I was paying for rent. Help kept coming from all sources. Before my visa expired, I had enough money to travel and fulfill my dreams. One week before my visa expired, I went to a shipping line to book one-way passage, third class, on Her Majesty Queen Elizabeth II luxury liner to New York City.

The first week of November, the ship departed from Southampton, England for the five day, seventeen hour voyage to New York with a two hour stop in Cherbourg, France to pick up more passengers.

After the ceremonious departure from Southampton, and having been four hours on the Atlantic Ocean, I decided to go to the library to read and to send post cards to my friends and relatives in London, Manchester City and Africa. Mysteriously, the only person in the library was a lady with ravishing beauty. She was a British lady. She must have been Celia Parsons but my conscious mind was not strong enough to pick it up. As I entered the library and our eyes met, she flashed a smile. It was so strong that the whole library became doubly illuminated. The British lady is an angel.

Layi: "Hello, angel. Do you have a pen?"

Celia: "Yes, I have one. You may have it."

Layi: "Thank you very much. Your generosity is highly appreciated."

Celia: "It is my pleasure."

Layi: "My name is Emanuel. You may call me Layi."

Celia: "My name is Celia Parsons." (And she started to walk out of the library).

Layi: "How will I return your pen to you?"

Celia: "I will see you tonight. Meet me at the lounge. I will be there at eight o'clock."

At exactly eight o'clock, I was at the lounge. Five minutes later, Celia joined me. She was gorgeously dressed; beautiful, five feet, seven inches tall, one hundred ten pounds. Her hair was at shoulder length, black, shining and flowing like silk.

Layi: "Hello, Celia. Are you going to dance?"

Celia: "No Layi, don't be silly. We are going to the movies. By the program "Doctor No" with James Bond is showing tonight and I want to see it with you."

In 1962, "Doctor No" was a popular movie and I was very happy that this gorgeous lady was going with me to see it. The wonderful night was just starting. After the movie, we took a walk to the top of the deck. The night was beautiful. The moon was full and shining brightly over the Atlantic Ocean.

We were on the deep ocean and her Majesty Queen Elizabeth II was cruising toward Cherbourg, France. In three hours, the ship was scheduled to arrive at Cherbourg. It was an unforgettable night, quiet, serene and very romantic. I thought it would never end. But, as soon as the ship arrived at Cherbourg, we went back to the lounge. Celia turned toward me. She put her arms around me and gave me a hug, a passionate kiss on my head and she quietly walked away from me.

When the ship, Her Majesty Queen Elizabeth II left Cherbourg, France, it was time for me to retire for the night. I was on Cloud Nine. I wished it would never end.

Finally, I had found real love. But, it was not conscious love. It was Celia Parsons' subconscious mind game. My five-day voyage from Cherbourg to New York City was very lonely and miserable. Celia was nowhere on the ship.

Two days later, I met a twenty-one-year-old beautiful black lady named Grace Hestes, a Jamaican born British lady, with ebony skin. She was gorgeous. I was willing to be with her rather than be alone on the ship. When her majesty Queen Elizabeth II left Cherbourg, France, I was on a high note. I fell in love with invisible Celia very deeply. I was definitely on Cloud Nine. I thought this good feeling would never end. I finally found a true love. But fortunately, this is not love, it is not conscious love, Celia operates only on a subconscious mind.

The following day, I went to the dining room for breakfast hoping to meet Celia. She had left and I would never see her again. I remember she once told me that "I am like a river, I flow in one direction and I continuously flow; no one has ever met me twice in one place."

I decided to make one more attempt. I went looking around for Celia. Instead, a black lady emerged. At first glance, I thought she must be Celia, but she couldn't be. Celia is a ravishing English beauty. The lady walking toward me is a beautiful black lady. Coming to the reality that I might not see Celia again, I decided to make a move to gain another companion.

Layi: "Good morning. my name if Layi. What is your name?"

Grace: "My name is Grace, Grace Hestes."

Layi: "Nice meting you, Grace."

Grace: "Likewise Layi."

Layi: "Grace, are you from London?"

Grace: "No. I am from Manchester City."

Layi: "I was in Manchester City two months ago. It is a beautiful city but very windy. Are you going to the U.S.A. for the first time?"

Grace: "I am going to New York for the first time. I am going to join my aunt who lives in Brooklyn. What about you? Do you know anybody in the U.S.A.?"

Layi: "I don't know anybody in New York. There is a family friend who is a student at Columbia University. He is not aware that I am coming to New York."

Grace: "Where are you going to stay in New York?"

Layi: "I have made an arrangement with the Y.M.C.A., William Sloan House at 360 West 34th Street. I am afraid I don't know how much the room costs and I don't have much money."

Grace: "Layi, don't worry. I will check you out. If you have financial problems, I can appeal to or request from my aunt to let you stay with us until you get a job."

Layi: "Thank you, Grace. What are you doing for the rest of the day?"

Grace: "Nothing."

Layi: "If you are not doing anything, can we do nothing together?"

Grace: "Fine, let us do it together."

Grace and I were together throughout the day and until late that night when we decided to go dancing. Everything was very romantic until a U.S. G.I., Allan Shepherd walked into the dance hall. He came to our table to request a dance with Grace. Of course, I could understand, there was a shortage of black ladies at the dance hall. Allan Shepherd took Grace away from my view for about one hour and when he finally brought her back to me, both of them apologized.

At the end of dancing, I walked Grace to her room, just like a gentleman. And before I left her room, I requested that meet me at the dining hall in the morning for breakfast. She accepted. The following morning at eight o'clock, I was at the dining hall waiting for Grace. One hour passed and there was no Grace. I decided to go to her room to find out what was delaying her. When I got to her room, I found Allan Shepherd and Grace together in Grace's bed in a romantic interlude. It was a great blow to my ego. I quietly left her room and it was the last time I saw Grace on the ship. The mystery continues.

Four days later, her Majesty Queen Elizabeth II reached her destination. With a sign of relief, I exclaimed, "New York City, here I come."

Having completed the immigration procedure, without wasting any more time, I took a taxi straight to the Y.M.C.A. on 34th Street in New York City. I began to realize that I was in a different world. "Déjà vu all over again." New York was heaven on earth.

The streets were very straight and wide. There were many luxurious large automobiles. People seemed to be taller on the average, and maybe they are trying to compete with the skyscrapers. The people of New York walked very fast and were always in a hurry. They didn't have time for one another. It was instant panic for me. I was not sure if I could survive in the City of New York.

When I arrived in London, I found London very slow and cold. The Londoners are as cold as their weather. New York is also cold, but New Yorkers are too hot to handle. When the taxi arrived at the Y.M.C.A., I paid the fare of two dollars. I could not afford the tip so I had to forgo it. The room was five dollars a night. The money I had on me could only last two weeks. If I didn't get a job in a hurry, I would be out on the streets. I checked into my room, but I could not rest. I picked the telephone up and dialed information to request my family friend's number, who lived on Broadway, near Columbia University.

Layi: "Operator, please do you have a telephone number for the Dejo Okediji on Broadway, New York City?"

Operator: "Just a moment please. I am sorry. Nothing is listed under the name."

Layi: "Thank you very much."

Operator: "You are very welcome. And, he hung up the phone."

I was surprised by the operator's answer: "You are very welcome." Maybe I was wrong about my opinion of New Yorkers not caring about anybody. The telephone operator just welcomed me to New York City. She didn't see me in person. How in the world did she know that I just arrived today?" Then, I picked up the telephone again to find out from her.

Layi: "Operator, good evening."

Operator: "Good evening. May I help you?"

Layi: "You welcomed me to New York. How did you know that I just arrived in New York today?"

Operator: "You arrived in New York today? From where did you arrive?"

Layi: "I arrived today from London."

Operator: "Okay. May I help you."

Layi: "I thought you knew that I just arrived—that is why you welcomed me."

Operator: But you just told me."

I realized that there was no communication between the operator and me. I had to hang up. I decided if I could not find our family friend's telephone number, I must walk to his house today to let him know that I am in the City. I knew I would need help. I just needed a job. I waited out in the street on Ninth Avenue and 34th Street. I was standing on the corner waiting to ask for directions. People were walking very fast and don't pay attention to anybody. Finally, I was able to talk to a lady. Please, how do I get to Broadway. She stopped and listened to me. She said, "Okay, you are on Ninth Avenue, go straight on 34th Street, the next is Eighth Avenue and the one after, that is Seventh Avenue and then Broadway, you can't miss it."

I looked at her and said thank you. Her answer was: "You are very welcome." Another surprise to me, why is everybody welcoming me in New York? Then it occurred to me that you are welcome is a common New York expression. I walked straight to Broadway from Ninth Avenue. On Broadway, I turned toward uptown, unaware that 34th Street to my friend's house on Broadway is not less than four miles. I started walking from six o'clock. I finally arrived at his house at nine o'clock. What a hard life, I was very tired. I was warmly welcomed. He put me in a taxi to take me back to the YMCA.

When I returned to my room, I was tired but I did not go to sleep right away. From ten o'clock p.m. to two o'clock a.m. I stuck my nose and eyeballs out of my window and for four hours I watched the busy 34th Street. As I watched people walking up and down the crowded street, I realized what was said about New York City is very true: this is the city that never sleeps. The streets of New York City are busy and crowded 24 hours a day, 365 days a year. This is the number one city in the world. I loved New York. Temporarily, I forgot all about my financial problems.

For the time being, I decided to enjoy my life like everybody else. My money problems went to the back burner. After two weeks, however, when the money for rent ran out, reality of life set in . Time to pay up or be pushed out on the street. I was about to be homeless until I mysteriously met a Nigerian Military Officer, Colonel Murtala Muhammed. He looked very handsome in his military uniform. In the early stage of Nigerian independence from Britain, Nigerians all over the world were very proud, patriotic and protective of each other. I knew very well that I would get some financial help from him. Also, I was very happy to see somebody from home. I followed him as he walked to the communication room to make a telephone call.

"Good afternoon, may I speak with the Consul General?"

"Who is calling?"

"Colonel Murtala Muhammad."

"Are you in trouble?"

"No, I am not in trouble," he said and hung up the telephone.

He was a very young military officer. He was confident with a commanding personality. I was not surprised that he later became Nigeria's Military Head of State. But, I was not intimidated, so I approached him.

Layi: "Hello Officer, my name is Babatunde. I am from Nigeria."

He responded to my approach. He was approachable and seemed very kind and personable.

Murtala: "Hello Babatunde. What are you doing here? Do you live here?"

Layi: "I arrived from London ten days ago. I have come here to go to school. I was accepted by the New York Institute of Photography. But, I have not started because my parents have yet to send me money. Actually, in two days my rent money will run out and I have no idea how I am going to continue." (He was very sympathetic to my story."

Murtala: "I am sorry. I don't like to see any Nigerian suffering in a foreign country. Come with me for lunch."

During the lunch, he explained to me that he was here in the U.S.A. for a short training with the U.S. Military. He wanted to spend one week in New York City, but there was an emergency. "I will be leaving tomorrow," he said. "My room is paid for twelve days. You can stay in my room for the remaining ten days. Give me a letter to your parents and I will deliver it to them."

General Murtala Muhammed saved me from being homeless. Later, our family friend, Dr. Dejo Okediji sent me more money and finally I got a job and became independent. So, my life in New York continued to the next stage. On Saturday afternoon, I received a telephone call. What a great surprise. It was Grace Hestes. I previously told Grace that I would be at the YMCA, 34th Street.

Grace: "How are you? This is Grace."

Layi: Grace, hello. Where are you?"

Grace: "I am in Brooklyn. Could you come have lunch with me on Sunday?"

Layi: "Yes, I would, at what time."

Grace: "At one o'clock, after church.

Layi: "Is two o'clock okay?"

Grace: "Two o'clock is okay."

Layi: "Please give me the address."

Grace: "Okay, I will see you on Sunday."

I became very happy. I thought I had lost Grace to Allan Shepherd forever. Grace was a very beautiful woman and I was very eager to see her again. But, on Sunday, when I arrived at Grace's for lunch, it was a disappointment because Allan Shepherd was also invited. He was there and I was very unhappy. It was a good lunch and I had an opportunity to meet Grace's aunt. She was a very wonderful person. I could not have intimate time with Grace because Allan Shepherd, as usual, took over. After a delicious meal, we left the dining room and assembled in their living room. Allan was still firmly in control. I took a magazine pretending to be reading. Toward the middle page was the pen pal section. The first name I saw was Wilma Browne, 16 years old; five feet and six inches tall; high school senior. Address: 16 Waring Street, Seaside, California. Then, I remembered Celia. This must be her. Before I left London, she told me I am in the book, look me up.

CHAPTER IV

Subconscious Mind

I have been to nearly two hundred cities and towns around the world. Everywhere I went, there was Celia's subconscious presence. Even in my conscious mind, she always resurfaced and mysteriously, I always followed.

One week after my dinner with Grace and Allan, I was invited to a party by Columbia University International Students at the International House on Riverside Drive, New York City. When I arrived at the party, I began to have strange feelings. I was lost, a complete stranger in a strange place. I felt all alone. There was no single familiar face. The music was booming and there was plenty of food to eat. People were laughing, eating and dancing. Everybody seemed happy. It was a very good party.

I was doing nothing, just standing by the wall, watching people enjoying themselves. But unconsciously, my mind seemed to be waiting for somebody to arrive. Fifteen minutes before midnight, there was an announcement made in the dance hall. "Ladies and gentlemen, the next song is going to be the last song of the evening so get your partners and make this an unforgettable night."

I looked around me, I was all alone. Everybody on the floor was engaged with one another as the music began to play. It was my favorite singer, Peggy Lee. A gorgeous lady appeared and she tapped my shoulder from behind. I turned toward her. She smiled and asked, "Shall we dance? I want to have the last dance with you."

"Sure, I'd love to," I answered. We danced for only five minutes. It seemed like one hour. This beautiful lady was an amazing kisser. She kissed me at the end of our dance. When I got home, I did not want to brush my teeth, hoping the taste of her tongue will remain forever in my mouth. It was my first kiss ever. After the dance, the strange ravishing beauty just vanished into the crowd. IT WAS A FLASH BACK!

I remembered mysterious Celia and her instructions to my subconscious mind: "I will meet you on board the H.M. Queen Elizabeth II. I will see you again at a party in New York City and I will attract you to California. I will be your pen pal. Write me, I am in the book."

I left Grace and Allan after the dinner with a smile on my face. I remembered in one of my mysterious encounters with Celia, she emphasized very strongly that when I arrived in New York City, I must get hold of a magazine and check the pen pal section. She said: "I am in the book, my name is Wilma Browne. You will find me and certainly, you will be with me in California. Just write me, you must keep the communication open and that is the bridge between us. You want to see me again? You must write."

I became confident that if I just wrote a letter I would see Celia again. I was very nervous. I did not know how to start. I did not know what to say in the letter. However, I started the letter.

Dear Wilma: My name is Layi Babatunde. I got your name from a magazine in New York City and I would like to be your pen pal. Thank you. P.S. I am twenty years old. I am originally from Nigeria. I lived in London briefly and also visited Manchester City where I met Celia. Do you know her? By the way, I saw her briefly on board the luxury ship Her Majesty Queen Elizabeth II where I spent five days and seventeen hours of voyage from Southampton, England to New York City. She is an English lady and she said she would be going to Seaside. I will be eagerly awaiting your reply. Thank you. Sincerely, Layi Babatunde.

Precisely one week later, my eagerly awaited reply arrived.

"Dear Layi: I love it. Your letter came as a surprise to me. Where did you get my name and my address? Anyway, let us forget about the details. I'd love to communicate with you and we will be friends. I am sixteen years old, a high school senior, and I live with my mother and younger brother, who is fourteen years old. My older sister, Shirley got married two years ago and she lives with her husband close by.

Seaside is a very small community in Monterey County in central California. We are a black family, originally from Dallas, Texas. My father died and our family moved to Seaside when I was eleven years old. We live by the sea. It is very beautiful here. If you happen to come here to visit me, I will take you around. Hoping to hear from you very soon. Truly yours, Wilma. P.S. I do not know Celia and I have never met any English people."

I was very happy to hear from Wilma Browne. But why and how is Celia connected to Wilma? The mystery of Celia continued. It seemed that I was chasing my own shadow. Looking back at the whole episode, it was like a movie shot in the Kalahari Desert titled, "The Gods Must Be Crazy."

However, I was more determined than ever before to solve the mystery of Celia, even if I had to leave everything else including my education. But first, I needed money. I must go and look for a job. I must make money to eat, pay my rent and to travel to California to visit Wilma Browne and also to continue to search for Celia.

Déjà vu all over again. I picked up The New York Times and checked the temporary section. Bingo, on the first page was Warren Temps, located at 80 Warren Street in downtown Manhattan between the Westside Highway and West Broadway. I paid one dollar for an eight-hour dish washing job. The pay was one dollar and fifty cents an hour. It was very early in the morning. It was a very cold December morning. The job was located only three blocks away, a restaurant on William Street, but I missed my way.

It was very cold, about ten degrees below freezing. I walked straight across the Brooklyn Bridge to the Williamsburg section of Brooklyn just to find that I had passed the restaurant by almost two miles. It was very cold. I did not even feel it, or I pretended not to. I needed the job and that was very important to me. I finally made it to the restaurant on time, eight o'clock.

I was well dressed. I had on a nice white shirt with a coat and a topcoat to match. Over dressed for a dishwashing job you might say. When I gave the introduction cards to the restaurant owner, he looked at me, smiled and asked, "Did you come to work or did you come to eat?"

Déjà vu all over again. I heard this expression when I was seeking a job at the London hotel. I answered, "I came to work," he smiled again and said, "Okay, follow me." He took me to the locker room and said here is your locker. Take off your coat and topcoat, put on this apron and meet me at the restaurant.

Before I got to the restaurant, he had already prepared a bucket of warm water for me to wash the windows. He asked me to go out in ten degrees below zero freezing cold weather to wash the windows. I quickly washed the windows, cleaner than when it was originally installed. After he inspected my job, he said, "Yes, you came to work."

I was only supposed to work for eight hours but he kept me working for him for one week totaling seven days. When my first job in America ended after one week, I had to look quickly for another job.

This time, it was relatively easy. I went back to 80 Warren Street Temps to buy another job. The down payment was ten dollars, with a total of one month's pay to be spread out over six monthly installments. Without hesitation, I gave ten dollars down payment and another job was given to me.

I was sent to a Jewish old peoples home on Saratoga Avenue in Brooklyn where I met the mother I never had, 60 year old Mrs. Aishman. She was the kitchen supervisor and a wonderful human being. Wherever she is now, I pray God put her soul in perfect peace. She employed me as a kitchen aid to make coffee and tea and to serve breakfast and lunch to the residents and wash dishes afterwards. Mrs. Aishman treated me as if I was her son. She made life easy for me. My job was very easy. I worked eight hours a day, seven days a week.

After working for six months, I decided to get a second job. This time, it was at the hospital as a janitor. It was very hard and had odd hours, from eleven at night to six in the morning. My regular job started at seven in the morning to three o'clock in the afternoon. I had two jobs.

In nine months, I saved enough money to make my way to California to meet my pen pal, Wilma Browne in person. We had been communicating regularly for eight months by letter and telephone calls two times a week. We were eventually going to fall in love. Subconsciously, I was communicating with Celia. It was Celia that I fell in love with. I continued to follow my shadow in search of Celia.

My journey to California was everything but smooth. It was long and tedious. On Friday night at ten o'clock, I took the Continental Trailways bus from the New York Port Authority to go across the United States. First to New Jersey, then straight to Pennsylvania, then non-stop to Ohio. With a brief stop, the journey continued to Indiana.

The bus continued cruising to Illinois. By mid-afternoon on Saturday, we were in Chicago. We had a two hour stop in Chicago to wash up, eat and change to another bus. The journey was just starting. The next call was Iowa, Nebraska and Colorado. We had traveled one full night and one full day, approximately fifty-six hours.

With just one short stop in Colorado, we continued an arrived in Salt Lake City, Utah. We headed on to Las Vegas, Nevada and finally, on Monday afternoon, we arrived at the final destination, Los Angeles, California. The journey took three nights, two days and twelve hours. When I finally arrived in California, there was a smile on my face. The weather was bright and cool, the air in Los Angeles in 1963) was fresh and smelled very sweet.

"I am home," I told myself. "Layi, you cannot get it better than this. I quickly settled in North Central, Los Angeles, 3622 Sixth Avenue became my new home. Later in the evening, after six hours of restful sleep, I decided to surprise my pen pal. All along, I kept my decision to come to California a secret. Before I left New York, I called her on the telephone to inform her that I may be taking a short trip out of New York and she should not write until she hears from me.

My telephone call from Los Angeles was a surprise as I expected it would be. But, she was very excited. When the phone rang, there was a female voice on the other side softly saying hello.

Layi: "Wilma, how are you? Guess where I am calling from?"

Voice: "No, this is not Wilma. This is Wilma's mother. Do you want to speak with Wilma?"

Layi: "Yes ma'am."

Wilma: "This is Wilma!"
Layi: "How are you, Wilma? Guess where I am calling from?"

Wilma: "You're calling from New York."

Layi: "No. Guess again."

Wilma: "I don't know. You should tell me."

Layi: "I am in California. Can I see you tonight?"

Wilma: "Where in California are you?"

Layi: "I am in Los Angeles."

Wilma: "Los Angeles? It is impossible. Are you insane? Los Angeles is four hundred miles from here. No, you cannot see me tonight."

Layi: "Okay, okay. Today is Monday. May I come to see you next Saturday?"

Wilma: "I will have to ask my mother if it is okay. Give me your telephone number. I will call you tomorrow night."

Layi: "Fine, call me tomorrow night."

I could hardly wait. I was in love with Wilma (supposedly disguised as Celia). That is what brought me to California, to see her in person. The following day Wilma called to let me know that her mother approved. I can come in two weeks. Then I realized that I must get a job right away. I need money for my rent, food and to travel to Seaside. On my second day in California, early in the morning, I set out to look for a job. It was my lucky day. Los Angeles employment office sent me to a department store, Harris and Frank in downtown Los Angeles. After a brief interview, I was employed as a stock clerk. After two weeks, the time had come for me to make a trip to Seaside to see my pen pal.

On Saturday morning at six o'clock, I took a Greyhound bus from Los Angeles to Seaside. It was a six hour ride. At ten o'clock, the bus arrived at the Seaside depot. There was Wilma waiting to meet me. Of course, we were both very nervous. We had never seen each other before. But immediately, I got out of the bus and we fell into each others arms. I was very excited and so was she. Wilma took me home to meet her mother, sister Shirley, and younger brother. It was a wonderful welcome. I felt right at home. After we had breakfast, Wilma and I decided to be alone. We went to the beach all day and at night we went to the movies. I was with Wilma throughout the weekend. I had to return to Los Angeles on Sunday. Wilma was the direct opposite of Celia Parsons. However, I decided to stay and be with her. Two months later, Wilma came to visit me in Los Angeles. Immediately after the visit, the magic was gone. There was no more interest on either side. We finally broke up. I then decided to forget about Wilma and Celia Parsons and concentrate on my goals. The following spring semester, I applied and enrolled at Los Angeles City College to study photography. I also joined the Democratic Party under the leadership of Jessie Unruh and my life continued.

CHAPTER V

A Prelude

In 1968, in Washington, D.C., the nation's capital, politics was in the air. President Lyndon B. Johnson had just announced to the world that he would not seek or accept the nomination of the Democratic Party for a second term of office. A few days later, the former attorney general and brother of beloved President John F. Kennedy, Robert announced his desire to run for the office of the Presidency. There was a sense of enthusiasm and excitement from the students attending various colleges and universities in California. I was one of them. And for me, the story began at this momentous time.

The year was 1968 and I was attending Los Angeles City College. I eagerly volunteered to campaign for Robert F. Kennedy. After all, he was one of my favorite politicians. He was my hero because as attorney general, he was the champion of Civil Rights. My assignment on primary election day was to go from door to door reminding people to go out and vote. On election night, the campaign staff and volunteers, including such notable football greats as Los Angeles Rams' Rosie Greer and River Johnson, gathered at the Ambassador Hotel Campaign Headquarters to await the election results. At about midnight when all the results were tallied, it was apparent that our candidate had won a landslide victory in the primary election. The music began to signal our celebration, but the jubilation was interrupted by the piercing sound of an assassin's bullet. Our candidate was murdered and the hotel was thrown into chaos and commotion. The party disintegrated into pandemonium. We had lost our candidate. We had lost our hero. Robert F. Kennedy died within a few hours of receiving the fatal bullets.

I lived about six miles away from the Ambassador Hotel. I had gone to the event that evening with a friend, another volunteer who promised to give me a ride home afterward. Unfortunately, this was not meant to happen. In the chaos at the campaign headquarters, I lost track of my friend. It was 2:00 a.m. in Los Angeles and public transportation was closed for the night. I did not have enough money to avail myself of taxi service. That night, I walked six miles to my apartment.

I had been attending Los Angeles City College and had just completed a two-year term. It was time for me to move on. My plan was to transfer to a four year institution but I was unclear about my true academic objectives. At City College, I studied a general curriculum of English, history, political science, psychology, anthropology and geology. I also took courses in photography. Although my grades were impressive, I was still dissatisfied.

In the summer of 1968, I decided to take one year off from my educational pursuits to earn some money. In the early hours of the fateful primary election day, I purchased the Los Angeles Times newspaper and perused the classified ads in search of employment opportunities. An ad for a shipping clerk caught my eye. Without wasting another minute, I went directly to apply for the position at Chrisali Fabrics on Santee Street in downtown Los Angeles. To support my application, I stated that I had two years experience in shipping. However, I was laid off when business declined. After submitting the application, I quickly returned to the campaign trail with no clue about the tragedy that would unfold that evening.

The day proceeded normally. I was assigned to work in the neighborhood where I lived. The work was not difficult since most people in the area already knew me. I received enthusiastic responses from Kennedy supporters. My home was on 30th Street, adjacent to Shrive Place Auditorium, and two blocks from the University of Southern California (USC). Some of the famous USC football players, including O.J. Simpson, also lived in my neighborhood.

I did not return to my apartment until early morning and even then, I could not sleep. I was tired, miserable and depressed. The tragic event that had occurred a few hours before kept replaying in my mind. At 10:00 a.m., I received a telephone call from Chrisali Fabrics to schedule an interview. In my groggy and zombie-like state, I heard a voice on the telephone say, "We have reviewed your job application. Can you come to our office at two o'clock to meet Yvette, the office manager for a final interview?"

At exactly two o'clock, I arrived at Yvette's office ready for my interview. Yvette pulled out my job application from the file and went through it thoroughly. "You have two years of college and you worked one year with Beach Mates of California as a shipping clerk and delivery agent, right?"

"Yes, that is correct."

"It seems from your college education and experience that you are quite qualified for the job. Do you have a driver's license?"

"Yes, yes I do," I answered. "Our company sells fabrics to the dress industry in the greater Los Angeles area. We generally ship our merchandise by United Parcel Service, but at times, you will be required to make personal deliveries to Santa Monica, Venice and Hollywood. The working hours are 8:00 a.m. to 5:00 p.m., daily from Monday through Friday.

"Oh yes, the pay is $5.00 per hour and you are allowed one hour for lunch. Are you still interested in this position, Layi?"

"Of course I am interested. When can I start," I inquired.

"Be here tomorrow morning at eight o'clock and I will introduce you to the staff members and get you started. Have a good evening."

The following morning, I reported to Yvette in eager anticipation of my new job. She gave me a tour of the office and warehouse and introduced me to the owner of the business. He was a tall, very distinguished European gentleman from Belgium. I also met the head of the sales department and then to my surprise, I was introduced to three gorgeous ladies. Carol, Evelyn and Elaine were professional graphic artists.

Their position was to design fabrics for dressmaker clients. Carol and Evelyn were Anglo Saxon and Elaine was Japanese American, born in Hawaii. They were so friendly. I began calling them "Designing Women." I admired them, but I was not interested in getting close to them. As I followed Yvette to her office for more instructions, a young, beautiful lady walked in.

"Good morning, Yvette," she said.

"Good morning Debby. Please meet the newest member of our warehouse staff."

"Hello, it's a pleasure to meet you," Debby said. "What is your name?"

"My name is Layi."

"Well Layi, I am the company secretary and you are going to be working closely with me."

From that moment, Debby and I seemed to have a common bond. We began taking our lunch together and normally would commute to work on the same bus. We were both black and after about three months on the job, everything seemed to be working well for Debby and me, or so I thought. I must have been losing my mind. I had planned to work for only one year, save money, then return to school to complete a degree. However, things changed after Debby and I met. I used all the money that I had been saving to buy a car just to please Debby. My college education took a backseat. For a very short time, we seemed to be happy.

One Friday evening, Debby and I made plans to go to Venice Beach to enjoy a nice dinner and then go dancing in Santa Monica. But, the evening was not meant to be. After work, I took Debby to her apartment and promised to return at seven to pick her up for our date. Upon returning, I parked the car and rang her doorbell. There was no response. Being somewhat concerned, I walk around the building and peeked through her window. I could see a romantic blue light in her bedroom and heard voices. I immediately recognized the sweet sound of Debby's voice, but who was the man?

My head filled with confusion and I began ringing the doorbell again, confident that I must be mistaken. I wasn't. Finally, Debby came to the door and opened it halfway to prevent me from entering. She looked at me and said, "I am sorry, but I cannot allow you to come in and I cannot go out with you tonight – or maybe, never again."

"What's going on?" I inquired. "My boyfriend has just returned from Viet Nam. I am sorry Layi."

That night I left Debby's house devastated and heartbroken.

That was the end of my journey with Debby. I went back to my own apartment and listened to music all night. It is amazing how powerfully healing music can be. I recovered from Debby quickly. It probably was no coincidence that my car also began to give me problems. One week after the breakup, I put my car in the shop for engine repair and resumed my routine on public transportation.

Help from the unexpected. In the evening after work, as I was walking to the bus stop I noticed a lady driving slowly behind me. She followed slowly until she arrived t the bus stop and I realized that I knew her. "Layi, where are you going and what happened to your car?"

"Hello Carol. My car developed engine problems and is in the shop. I'll be riding the bus for another week."

"Well, hop in and let me give you a lift," she offered.

Carol lived in the very affluent area of Venice, a good eight miles from my home. I was surprised of her offer, yet grateful. When we arrived at my apartment, I thanked her for the kind act. At this point, the surprise continued when she volunteered to pick me up in the morning and drive me to work. Although I appreciated the gesture, I declined, not wanting to put her so far out of her way. But, every evening after work, Carol insisted on driving me home. When my car was finally repaired, so was my attitude about people. Even my perception toward racial issues had changed. Carol's extension of friendship bridges the cultural and racial divide.

My other employer, two summers before, Beach Mates of California, had employed me. The company manufactured and distributed swimwear throughout the western United States and Hawaii. The owners, Sid and Thelma Liroff, were helpful and kind. My job was terminated, however, because of declining business.

Now that I was back on the road, I decided to stop in and visit with them one afternoon. The couple seemed genuinely happy to see me and asked me to consider returning to their company. Although I was quite content with Chrisali Fabrics, the financial incentives favored a move. I accepted the offer with the understanding that they would allow me one week's notice to my present employer. It was difficult for me to leave Chrisali. I loved working with Yvette, Carol and Elaine. Our friendships were solid. When we said our farewells, we all promised to keep in touch. I did not bother to inform Debby about my departure. We had already said good-bye.

Carol, Evelyn and Elaine My ladies kept their promise to keep in touch with me. We talked on the telephone weekly and while making deliveries in their neighborhood, I usually stopped in for a brief visit. Sometimes, even for lunch. Elaine called me one day and mentioned that she would be traveling to Hawaii to spend Christmas with her family. I jokingly invited myself along with her and she very pleasantly acquiesced. Instead of joining her, however, I asked that she bring me a University of Hawaii catalogue. Two weeks later, Elaine returned to Los Angeles with the catalogue in hand. When I looked through the manual, I was impressed and especially interested in the College of Business Administration programs. Elaine was a graduate of the University of Hawaii, so she enthusiastically endorsed the school. I decided to try it out for a summer school program.

Evelyn moved back to the East Coast. In early January of 1969, Evelyn announced that she was moving back to Pennsylvania. But before leaving, she wanted to host a farewell dinner at her home Evelyn lived in Far Corner, a very exclusive area of Los Angeles. Carol called me to inform me about the dinner plans and asked if I would be able to attend. Since I had always seemed to get lost when traveling in that neighborhood, Carol suggested that we ride together. She picked me up at four o'clock for the event. Although Elaine was unable to attend, we enjoyed an intimate gourmet dinner which Evelyn had prepared. It would be the last time I saw Evelyn.

Elaine's Engagement Party. February brought a different reason for celebration. Elaine got engaged and a party was planned in her honor. It was a small party for a few close friends. Once again, I was plagued with car problems so I prevailed upon Carol to give me a ride. Her schedule was complicated but she agreed to bring me home if I could find alternative transportation to the dinner. I could not find anyone to drive me to the dinner but I was determined to attend even if I had to go by taxi. As I got ready and was about to call for a taxi, the telephone rang. It was my friend, Mr. M.G. Kasali (RIP) who lived in my building. Thinking that the time of the call was very fortuitous, I quickly asked him to give me a ride to the party. He agreed to pick me up in thirty minutes and take me to Elaine's home in Santa Monica.

With luck on my side, I arrived at the dinner party on time but I was surprised to find only four other people in attendance. We were a total of five, Elaine and her fiancé, Carol, myself and another lady introduced as Celia. There were the perfunctory greetings, and I extended my hand to Celia. She reached out and we shook hands, but as our eyes met in a mystifying gaze, she moved back about ten steps. It was as though some paranormal force caused her retraction.

Celia was very slim, but not thin. She stood about 5' 7" and weighed approximately 110 lbs. She was nicely built, albeit slightly high shouldered. Her straight black hair danced on her shoulders. She was young, beautiful and with an angelic countenance. She reminded me of someone I had met before.

Several years ago, I was on board the luxurious ocean liner, Queen Elizabeth II (QE II), five days and seventeen hours into a voyage from Southampton England to New York City. I was alone in my cabin, very bored and lonely. I decided to go to an upper deck for some fresh air. The sun had already faded into the west and the moon shone brightly over the Atlantic Ocean. The water glistened and our vessel was cruising majestically and royally just like the queen she was. It was the most beautiful sight I had ever seen.

We were scheduled to stop briefly in France to receive more passengers for our non-stop journey to the United States. Upon embarkation in the Port of France, I decided to wander through the souvenir shop in search of post cards. I had many friends to communicate with in London, Manchester and Lagos. After purchasing three cards, I strolled to the library to find a comfortable location for writing. The library cabin is quiet and welcoming. I found the perfect overstuffed chair before realizing I had no writing instrument. I turned slightly in hope of finding a neighbor who might spare a pen. My eyes became instantly fixed on a beautiful lady alone at a desk writing cards, as had been my mission.

I watched her as she continued her task, unable to speak. Finally, when it appeared that she was preparing to leave, I was compelled to address her. As if reading my thoughts, she looked directly at me and smiled knowingly.

"Hello," I spoke barely above a whisper. "I see you are sending some postcards. I was about to do the same thing."

"Yes, I am," she returned. "May I ask where you are from?"

"I'm sorry. My name is Layi," I extended my hand toward her.

She graciously accepted my gesture and said, "I am from Manchester City and my name is Celia."

Once formalities were behind us, we found ourselves engaged in warm, friendly but unobtrusive conversation. We were both traveling alone it seemed. I needed a pen and she offered me hers. After exchanging brief information about how we both happened upon this excursion, she very politely excused herself and walked out of my life. But, I could not get her out of my head. I carried her pen daily and hoped that our paths would again cross. With more than one thousand passengers traveling on this great lady, what were the prospects of meeting Celia, Celia Parsons once more?

After five days, my hopes were waning. There was no glimpse of Celia. As I was leaving he dinner room on our sixth night, I happened to meet a stunning Jamaican lady. She was born in London and was en route to New York for the first time. I was thrilled to have met her and she seemed equally happy to have company. In fact, she offered her cabin number and suggested that I meet her later that evening.

When I arrived at her cabin, she welcomed me with the same grace as before. Innocuous chatting was followed by a foray to the disco. We danced until nearly dawn. No subsequent plans were discussed as I ushered her home. No invitation to spend more time was proffered. While floating to my cabin on the cloud she had given me, I fantasized about our next meeting. It happened to be at breakfast where I saw her visiting with an African-American GI. She didn't notice that I noticed and I never saw her again.

The remainder of my trip to New York was nothing short of miserable. The pain suffered during the balance of the trip was only exceeded by my first six months in the Big Apple. It wasn't my first trip.

Fortunately, I had some friends who indulged in my despair. There was a party being organized at the International Center on Riverside Drive. It was scheduled for Saturday night. Of course, I could attend. It would interrupt my self-pity, but the diversion might be healthy.

I arrived about 10:00 p.m. To my surprise, the Center was packed with people. There was plenty of music, gaiety ad the food was delicious. Even though I truly had a passion for dancing, I was determined to be resolute in my misery. I stood alone in a remote corner of the room and simply watched the fun going on. As the venue for the last dance was set, I sensed someone staring at me. It was a wildly familiar sensation and I turned slightly to meet the eyes of a beautiful woman.

She approached me and extended her hand without saying a word. I followed her to the dance floor for the last dance, my first of the evening. The song was Peggy Lee's "Fever." I felt it. She moved very close and tight against my body and we began to melt into each other. This strangely familiar stranger looked straight into my eyes and my mouth reached for her lips. It was a long and passionate kiss. It was my first ever.

The music stopped and I spoke. "Thank you for the dance. You are an angel. Do you live in New York City?"

"No, I am from London, actually, Manchester City."

"Have we met? Do you know?

"I live in Chicago now. It's very cold and windy, just like home. Have you ever been to Chicago?"

"I was there for a few weeks in 1962."

"Well then, you know how cold it can be. Enough about me. Let's talk about you. Where were you born? Tell me about your family. Just tell me everything?" Her tone was commanding.

"All right Celia, I will tell you everything if you really want to know. But remember that you should only ask about what you really want to know.

"I was born in Oyo, Nigeria. I am sure you know that Nigeria is a former British Colony. Oyo Empire stretches from the River Niger to the north of the Atlantic Ocean in the south from Jebba to Porto Novvo Benin Republic. Aalafin, the King, was the head and ruler of Oyo Empire. Aalafin is generally known as Oba Kabiyes, Iku-Babayeye Aalafin of Oyo. The Aalafin council of ministers consists of seven hereditary chiefs knows as Oyo 'mesi.' Alphabetically, these are Aare-Ago, Alapinni, Akin-niku, Qashipa, Bashorun, Lagunna and Saa-owu.

"Bashorun is the prime minister and my maternal grand-mother was heir to Bashorun's throne. My father was a distant cousin to Ashipa. My paternal grandmother was first cousin to Alapinni. My parents had a very rich and prestigious heritage and were heirs to many natural resources but money was scarce. From my fourth birthday, I had three goals in life: to get an education, to travel and know the world, and to become very rich. My parents also understood my dream so they asked my uncle to take me to live with relatives in Lagos, to assure me of a quality education. I was fortunate. I grew up in a good Christian home where I was encouraged to work hard to achieve my goals."

I told Celia everything I could think of, including my life in London. My sister was already there. She came to meet me at Victoria Station to deliver me to my cousin in Clapham Common in north-west London. It was autumn, yet very cold for me. The climate in London was very different from my home in Lagos. I missed home and my friends. Thankfully, my cousin and his wife embraced me and I was able to readjust in short order. I went to apply for employment after six months, and was hired the same day. The only job available was as a dishwasher at the New Cavendish Hotel. It was a difficult job for me but I had no other choice. I needed money on which to live and to attend school. After working only two weeks, I was fired. The reason was never made clear to me; incompetence, race, just not good enough? No matter, I set out to find another position. My next job was in a warehouse at the Chase Clampton in Clampton North, North-west London. I was hired on the spot. The business was primarily trade in films, cameras, projectors and photographic materials. I liked the company and liked my job.

Now, it was time for me to locate a place to stay. It was time to move out of my cousin's house and become independent. It was not an easy task. My weekly income was only $18.00. I knew that I could afford only a small room but I was not aware that the conditions of residency were more costly: "No Colored, no Irish, no dogs," the ads repeated.I kept looking diligently but ultimately faced the same discrimination. Although this attitude was foreign to me, I did not permit myself to become discouraged. My only possibility became a small room involving a four-hour per day commute to my job. I took the accommodation.

It was several weeks before I received a telephone call from a family friend. It was to inform me that a room was available in Islington, northwest London. An Irish person owned the house so there was no fear of rejection. I leapt at the opportunity and made an appointment to see the room. It was located in an attic; very small but clean. The cooking facilities were adequate and most importantly, it was located very close to my job, only a thirty-minute ride by Tube. I relocated the following weekend and was very happy in my new digs.

Settled happily in my new home, with my good job, I had no more reasons not to plan for my primary objective, schooling. Since I had come to enjoy working with photographic equipment, I decided to enroll in the London School of Cinema to study photography and film editing. The year was 1961. I was inspired. After only six months, I dropped out of the program. I did not, however, lose my interest in photography. I happened across some information on the New York School of Photography and I responded by submitting an application. I was accepted into the school and embarked on a journey via the Queen Elizabeth II.

Celia listened intently, interested in my story. Strangely intrigued by the tale, she never questioned or interrupted me. She appeared mesmerized by the story, or was it I who was mesmerized? How amazing that I could fit almost my whole life story into a thirty minute interval? I paused and surrendered my gaze to the overwhelming power of her countenance until the silence was broken.

"I enjoyed the dance but I have to go."

"Wait. Please wait. Just tell me your name again. Please."

"Celia, Celia Parsons. Good night Layi."

My head was spinning. First the QE II, then the International Center. We danced, we kissed, it was the first time my lips had ever felt a woman's touch. In all figurative manners, my virginity was lost forever. I gave her my story and together we became the epitaph. It was Celia before. Was it Celia now at Elaine's engagement party?

CHAPTER VI

It Begins

Celia and I returned to the group. Carol, Elaine and her fiancé were engrossed in a game of Monopoly. The game continued until almost four o'clock in the morning. When it was finally time to go home, everyone bid farewell and thanked the host and hostess for the wonderful evening. Carol offered both Celia and me a ride home. My apartment was logistically the first drop-off point. When we arrived at my place, I stepped out of the car and turned to address Celia.

"Nice meeting you. Maybe we can get together again sometime." It was trite, but it was all I could think of at the time.
"Here's my phone number, call me."

I was surprised and encouraged by Celia's quick response. The night proved to be the last time I would see Carol and Elaine, but it was the beginning of my relationship with Celia.

Mystery Lady. It was Sunday morning and I awakened around eight. The sun was shining through my window and I could hear birds singing. I glanced at the table next to my bed and saw the piece of paper with Celia's phone number. After a warm shower and a nice breakfast, I got ready to attend church. It was my normal Sunday routine. And just as typical was my sense of boredom when I returned after the service. Sunday can provide an element of rejuvenation for weary souls, but my soul was still restless. The excitement of the prior evening kept me feeling on edge. I looked over at the same nightstand beside my bed, and the paper with Celia's number was still waiting for me. I acquiesced and dialed the number.

"Good morning, YWCA. May I direct your call?"

The voice was friendly, yet officious. "Thank you. May I speak with Celia?" I asked. "She is in room 18D, one moment please."

It seemed like an hour until I heard the sweet voice answer,

"Good morning, this is Celia."

"Hello. This is Layi. Do you remember me?

"How could I not, Mr. Nigeria?"

"Shall I call you Miss England or Miss Manchester City?

"Please call me Celia."

"Okay, Celia. How are you?

"I am very well, Layi. How are you this beautiful morning?"

"Well, to be perfectly honest Celia, since I set my eyes on you, I have not been able to stop thinking about you. I just wanted to... well I do need to know if you feel the same way about me."

"I've been able to think of little else Layi. If you are free today, why don't you come down for a visit?"

"I have nothing planned Celia and would like nothing more. I'll see you around six."

Having just retrieved my car from yet another mechanical nightmare, it was fortuitous that I could be back on the road for my rendezvous with Celia. The YWCA hostel was about fifteen minutes from my home without traffic congestion. Celia was in the reception area waiting for me at six o'clock. She greeted me with an angelic smile; contained emotion, yet deep. She was at that moment, my own private lady angel and I was ready to embrace her as my own heavenly goddess. We shared the most beautiful three hours of my life that single Sunday evening.

Four short months before my inevitable departure to Honolulu, Celia and I started dating. Prior to meeting Celia, Carol and Elaine were my best friends. They were responsible for introducing me to Celia. Sometimes I felt that I had abandoned them for her. In reality though, I came to believe that their primary purpose in my life might have been just to bring Celia and me together. Celia represented more than a friendship. She became my lover, my confidant and my guardian. Whether by design or accident, we were together. I had not one iota of doubt in my heart that our relationship would last forever. Celia, after all, was everything that any man would dream of, love to have, and perhaps die for. Just as I knew she descended from heaven just for me, I was confident of the strength and longevity of our union.

But, again I was wrong. Torrid passion tempered by gentle touching turned icy within three months. It was almost time for me to leave for the University of Hawaii. Celia was fulfilled and finished. Whatever she had desired had been satiated. Without warning or farewell, she seemed to vanish. But not completely gone. Her mystique became a permanent part of my life. The saga of our relationship was really just beginning.

Exactly one week before my departure, I spent the entire day in the library of the University of Southern California. I was busying myself with research and in preparation for my imminent academic launch. Although I knew that my educational pursuit at last needed to come first, on this particular day I was longing for my love. All that I really wanted to do was to be with Celia if only once more. I picked up the telephone to call her. A sweet, familiar voice answered.

"Hello Celia."

"No, I am Kayleen."

"May I speak with Celia please?"

"Wrong number. I am sorry, but no Celia lives here."

It was curt and cutting. What had happened to my Celia? It sounded like her yet I couldn't be absolutely certain. Was this some kind of tortuous game? I waited about thirty minutes and dialed the number again. her response was the same. My mind was in turmoil and my heart was pounding. I had to know more about what was happening to me. I had to know what happened to us. What wretched circumstance would perpetuate this level of deceit? I decided to call again. Again, Kayleen identified herself. I asked her to meet me for dinner and much to may amazement, she accepted the invitation. My imagination was running wild. Could Kayleen actually be Celia? If she was playing games with me, why? Could she be angry with me for not fully disclosing my plan to leave Los Angeles and return to school? Or, was she simply finished with me? I hoped to find out at dinner on Wednesday evening.

On time, and with much anticipation, I drove to the YWCA hostel to have dinner with the woman I hoped would be my Celia. As I parked the car and prepared to get out, a woman approached me straight away. My hopes faded. The lady was not Celia. The only thing physically in common was that both women were Caucasian.

"Are you Layi," she inquired.

"Yes, my name is Layi. Would you be ....?

"Good evening. my name is Kayleen."

Kayleen was very petite, 4'9" tall and weighed about 100 lbs. Her hair was cropped short and was coal black. Her eyes were green and her attire was stunning. No, she definitely wasn't Celia, but she was equally gorgeous.

"I'm happy to meet you Kayleen. Are you ready for dinner?"

"Oh yes. If you don't have anything in mind, I know a nice Greek restaurant in Santa Monica. Do you like Greek food Layi?"

"That sounds great. Let's go there."

We drove to her suggested spot and enjoyed a delicious meal. Kayleen's company was very pleasant. She was extremely intelligent and we conversed on various general topics. Although I initiated the invitation to determine a connection with Celia, I must admit that asking her questions about Celia did not cross my mind at dinner. In fact, we both avoided any discussion of a personal nature but there was absolutely no tension between us. I mentioned to her that I was leaving for Hawaii in less than a week, and vowed to keep in touch with her. At the end of a very pleasant and innocuous evening, I returned her to the hostel and bid her good night. I felt a sense of tranquility and closure as I began to focus on the tasks to be completed before my departure.

June 12, 1969 came quickly. I left Los Angeles to begin my college career at the University of Hawaii. My five-hour flight over the Pacific onboard the "Friendly Skies" was safe and smooth. The moment the plane touched down at Honolulu Airport, I was warmed by the tropical breezes and intoxicated by the scent of the lush floral landscape around me. At that moment, I knew that I was home. Not so surprising, my homeland of Nigeria looked very much like the environment around me. I gave myself permission to be still and soak up the power of the place. I allowed myself to remember home and in doing so I began to feel at home. This enabled me to be comfortable about where I was so that I could begin to forge the path to my destiny.

All around me people were being greeted and adorned with leis of plumeria, hibiscus and sweet island rose. Hawaii is uniquely hospitable and the people of Hawaii are the friendliest I have ever met. In Hawaii, the color of your skin does not matter. Here, there are beautiful combinations of skin colors, all shades of brown, yellow, black and white. Hawaii is much of a melting pot. This tropical paradise is on a zone that does not possess the harsh environment that is typical of the tropics.

No person was there to meet me. I knew no one on the island. I had contacted the YMCA near the University campus to request accommodation assistance. I received no response but was confident there would be a place for me upon my arrival there. I quickly called a taxicab and went to the YMCA located on University Avenue.

As expected, a room awaited me. It was a very small clean room with bunk beds for two residents. The nightly rate included linens, towels, and community bathroom facilities. I was the first to check in so I claimed the lower bed. I was anxious to unpack and get back outside to explore my new surroundings.

I walked out to the front of the building which opened to the University campus. I saw a black gentleman unpacking his car, preparing to enter the building. He also noticed me and I was thankful that he approached me.

"Good afternoon, are you new around here" he inquired.

"Yes. I arrived today. Do you attend the University or are you visiting?"

"I came to attend the University."

"Welcome. My name is Jeffrey and I am a junior in the College of Tropical Agriculture. I am from Cameroon."

"Nice meeting you Jeffrey, my name is Layi. I came here from California, but I am originally from Nigeria. I am also going to be a junior this fall in the College of Business Administration. The climate in Hawaii is so similar to Africa and this city is a paradise."

"The campus is also beautiful Layi. I think you'll enjoy being here."

"Would you like to take a drive around town?"

"Sure. Thank you Jeffrey. That would be great!"

We drove through Honolulu. It truly was a wonder city. Well planned and clean. Mango and coco palm trees flanked both sides of the main thoroughfares. The people were beautiful, brown and very friendly. We traveled from Kapiolani Beach to Kailua and finally to Waikki Beach. At Waikki, there were people from all over the world. It was truly a multicultural array of red, black, white, yellow and sepia faces against a backdrop of azure Pacific Ocean eventually meeting an even bluer sky. I was humbled at the vision. For whatever reason, I became overwhelmed with angst about Celia. I missed her so very much and the beauty of the setting before me only exacerbated the feeling of her absence. For a moment the colors around me faded and I stood alone on the beach, staring at a horizon with no beginning and no end.

When we returned to the hostel, my new roommate had already arrived. David Phu was a young Chinese man from Berkeley, California. He was to become my comrade throughout my University experience. At the moment though, I just felt fortunate to have found a friendly companion. The following day, I went to the University bookstore and purchased three postcards to send to special people back on the mainland: very special people like Celia, Kayleen and my very good and beautiful Mexican friend, Graciella Delatre. I wrote just a little note to say hello, with the exception of Celia. On her card, I spoke of the natural paradise that God created called Hawaii. I told her that she would forever regret failing to visit here to become part of the beauty, even if only for a moment. Alas, I received no response from Celia or either of the other ladies. My life went on.

My schedule at the University was smooth and simple. I registered for only two courses the first semester, English and Business Management. While on campus, I remembered that Elaine mentioned to me that her brother was a lecturer in the College of Education. I promised her that I would definitely make his acquaintance. One day on the way to find him in the College of Education building, I observed a woman in the courtyard who resembled Celia. She was the same height and displayed nearly identical mannerisms. From a distance, I watched her before I decided to approach.

"Hello. I'm new here, please. Could you direct me to the college of Education?"

She pleasantly responded, "Sure, follow me, that's where I'm going."

"Who do you want to see there?" "

I'm looking for Dr. David Gima. Do you know him," I inquired?

"Sure, I know him. I'll take you there."

I couldn't believe how much she reminded me of my lost love. She took me to Dr. Gima, who fortunately had been notified by Elaine of my enrollment. He greeted me warmly and offered to take me to lunch.

My friendly guide was about to leave before I could express my appreciation.

"Excuse me," I blurted out without hesitation. "Thank you for helping me find my way. I'm in your debt. What is your name?"

"Oh, you're quite welcome. Good luck here at the University". She turned briefly to look back at me as she walked away. "My name is Celia."

Dr. Gima proved to be a very valued and cherished island resource. On our first lunch, he introduced me to a high school principal from Waimea High School on the island of Kaui. Dr. "RIP" Ho was a hospitable man. He invited David and me to visit his family in Kauai.

With much gratitude and absolutely no hesitation, we graciously accepted the invitation and prepared for our weekend holiday.

Kauai is known as the "Garden Isle" because of the lush tropical foliage. Rainbows, waterfalls, caves and white beaches garish the beauty of flowers, trees and rainforests. With Dr. Ho's clan we were treated to a tour of the island in "native" style: by boat and on foot. We explored the hidden treasures of Kauai until it was time to return to Honolulu.

The first day of summer school was pretty routine and my schedule was light. I was free every afternoon. Following this first day of regular classes, I was sitting in the hostel's restaurant enjoying lunch. Soon David also finished for the day and still elated from the holiday in Kauai, entered the room and suggested we go for a swim at the campus pool. I have never been a swimmer but the water sounded refreshing and I felt game.

We arrived at the facility early in the afternoon. David jumped in the water and I followed. I don't know how to swim. In a fraction of a second, I lost touch with myself. I felt myself sinking and realized that I must be drowning. I was calm, my body was calm and I felt myself moving away from the restriction of my physical form. The experience was as fluid as the water around me. I was out of my body and moving toward a very large gate. There was an amazingly brilliant light ahead of me and I wanted to walk into the beckoning luminary. I wished to become it. As I moved nearer and nearer it seemed that I could only have been a few feet away from the entrance.

Suddenly, somehow, out of the elements before, Celia materialized in front of me. She blocked my path and turned me around. It was as if I had no control over her power, because I wanted to go forward. It was painful but she was sending me back to my body. When I regained consciousness I was in the emergency room at Queens Medical Center in Honolulu. Several doctors were around me and I could see David in the background. But nowhere around me was the person responsible for bringing me back. Celia had once again eluded me.

CHAPTER VII

Los Angeles Revisited

When Celia and I were dating, she was a warm and gentle woman. Despite the obvious racial differences, background and culture, I felt we were the proverbial "match made in heaven." I was very happy yet something was wrong.

I might have taken her for granted and if that were so, I am sorry. Celia left me without warning or goodbye. Everywhere I tuned, consciously or unconsciously, she was always in my thoughts. My obsession with her made it extremely difficult even impossible to have a relationship with another woman. I began to have recurring dreams and out of body experiences. These sensations repeatedly gave me visions of Celia impregnated with my child. I saw her wandering in places I couldn't recognize. I hoped that she was somehow seeking me but I could never travel close enough to touch her. Was it love or punishment? She seemed to be completely taking over my life, a life that had become empty, miserable and lonely.

Historically, it has never been difficult for me to meet people or to make friends. I consider myself somewhat of a ladies man. One quiet Friday evening, exactly three weeks after my near death experience at the University swimming pool, I sat alone in the YMCA hostel. Victor Askement and Noel Francisco, my normal television buddies were out on dates with their girlfriends. I was alone with nothing to do. My life was boring.

I stared through the window into the darkness, which was boldly interrupted by the light of a full moon. I decided to go outside and enjoy the celestial display. No sooner had I stepped outside on University Avenue, a lady appeared in my peripheral vision. She seemed to emerge out of the blackness of the night, yet haloed by the radiance of the moon. She was dressed in a loose flowing gown with flowing shoulder length straight black hair. She carried a flute and was approaching me in an almost goddess like splendor. I stopped in my tracks and waited for her to reach me.

"Can you give me directions to the music building?" she asked.

"Yes. I was thankful to have someone with whom to converse. It's just down the street. I can take you there if you'd like."

"You are very kind," she responded.

As we began walking down University Avenue toward the music building, she sighted a garden display of tropical flowers. She was especially intrigued with the Birds of Paradise. We stopped by the plantings and sat down. No words were spoken between us. We appeared to be communicating on another level. It was as if she were meditating with the flowers. Birds of Paradise are particularly fascinating and beautiful in the moonlight. After approximately thirty minutes had passed, she looked at me and thanked me for being with her. I told her that I enjoyed her company and we again embarked upon our destination to the music building. Almost as mysteriously, she stopped again and this time pointed to our left.

"What's up there?" she asked.

"That is the amphitheater," I told her.

"It looks so beautiful. Can we go there and have a look around?"

Of course, I was only too pleased to accompany this lady. The full moon was shining brightly and the entire theater adopted its magical aura. We went inside the gates and there was no other soul in sight. She moved to the center of the facility and sat down, beckoning me to sit close beside her. Without conversation, she raised her flute and began to play my favorite song, "Fever," made famous by Peggy Lee.

Momentarily, I was entranced. The music suddenly returned me to Riverside Drive in New York City where I danced to the same music and savored my first kiss with Celia. This beautiful creature played the same tune, with eerie familiarity. At the end of the song, she looked at me and smiled. She relaxed and moved very close to me, adjusting her dress just enough to expose her breast. She looked flawless in the moonlight and I was becoming very excited. She further teased me by reaching for my hand and laying it gently upon her breast. As if following her orchestration, I reached toward her lips for a sweet kiss.

The spell was instantly broken as she pushed me away. She scolded me for wanting her. She chided my cultural background, lack of good judgment and begged us to return to the hostel. In amazement, I acquiesced. Still very dazed and confused, I walked her back to the spot of our meeting. We sat down on a bench outside the building and she again took out her flute and played another tune. This time, she played "Up, Up and Away," by the Fifth Dimension. I was impressed with her talent but her sting left me paralyzed. At the end of this performance, she stood up and thanked me again.

"I enjoyed your company too," I managed to speak. "What is your name?"

"Don't worry about my name. I am leaving for Los Angeles early tomorrow morning. We may never meet again. But if you happen to be in L.A., look me up at the YWCA hostel downtown. I stay in room 18D."

With that, she disappeared into the building. I was lost in déjà vu. The mention of the Los Angeles YWCA hostel returned me to memories of Celia. Thoughts of her catapulted me back to her arms. I needed to return to L.A. I had to see the beautiful creature that played for me. Perhaps she appeared only to lead me back to Celia. Perhaps she was Celia incarnate.

Alas, it was the middle of the school semester and I could not abandon my studies. I was on a mission. I had to wait until the end of the current term. On December 14th, two days after final examinations, I was as free as a bird and boarded the "Friendly Skies" back to Los Angeles. I returned to my old address where I stayed with Mr. MC. Kasali. Fortunately, he was traveling in Africa so his apartment was available for my accommodation. I had only four weeks for Christmas vacation, after which I would be compelled to return to Honolulu for the spring semester. While in L.A., I planned to work at one of two job opportunities awaiting me. Before I left California, Gene Corlins, with whom I worked at Beach Mates of California and later at his own business invited me over for a bon voyage dinner. He and his beautiful daughter, Patricia, hosted me and invited me to work with them again if I ever returned to the Los

Angeles area. Even if just for a holiday, they assured me that a position would always be open for me.

Other people in Los Angeles were also friendly toward me, people like the Liroff's, who owned the Beach Mates business. In fact, even after I left for school, they stayed in contact with me. Two months after my arrival in Hawaii they took a holiday there and to my surprise they came to the University to look me up. They invited me to their hotel for dinner and promised to pick me up after school on Friday at six o'clock. Instead, they sent a limousine to get me and take me to the Kahala Hilton Hotel. My friends were staying at the best hotel in Honolulu. All royal dignitaries stay at the Kahala Hilton upon arrival on Oahu.

It was a perfect evening in paradise. Tropical breezes, close friends, and exquisite cuisine made the dinner party wonderful. Mrs. Liroff even packed leftover food for me to take back to my dormitory. She treated me as a son and I relished the nurturing. As we said good night, they both reiterated my welcome, should I ever decide to return to California.

Now that I was back in town for four weeks, I made the decision to work for Beach Mates. Once I became reacquainted with my terrain, I finally decided to visit the mysterious lady at the YWCA in room 18D. I telephoned the hostel and requested to be connected with room 18D. The person who answered was neither Celia nor the enchanted lady with the flute. It was Kayleen's voice I heard. I quickly determined that inquiries would not be appropriate at this time, so I went straight to the point.

"Good evening, Kayleen. This is Layi."

"Hello, Layi. When did you come back to L.A. or are you calling from Honolulu?"

"I returned last week. I wasn't sure you were still at the YWCA hostel. Would you like to have lunch, dinner or go to the movies?" I asked.

"Let's have dinner. How about Friday evening? I can pick you up."

She was quick to accept my invitation.

On Friday evening Kayleen arrived to pick me up for dinner. But instead of going out for diner, she had a different idea. She wanted us to stay home and call for Golden Bird Dinner delivery. She stayed with me all evening. It was a pleasant and cordial conversation until nearly 1:00 a.m. When Kayleen was leaving she gave me a new telephone number and asked me not to call her any longer at the YWCA hostel, room 18D.

Two days later, I called the new telephone number. As seemed to be becoming a pattern with women in my life, Kayleen was distant and cold. It didn't please me that I was actually getting accustomed to this game. But I really needed to learn the rules of engagement. The mysteries surrounding bizarre female activity were like a crank worm eating deeply into my heart. I returned to Honolulu to resume school.

Despite her disinterest, I made another attempt to correspond with Kayleen, but there was no response. Ironically, while I waited in anticipation of Kayleen's reply, I received a letter from Celia. Thank God her reality was confirmed. Countless times, I questioned my sanity about this elusive lady who seemed to weave some kind of common thread throughout my subsequent relationships.

Celia's letter was simple yet obtuse. She wished me good luck in my studies and reminded me of words that she had spoken to me several times before, "Remember me if you become somebody important!" The puzzle, of course, is how "important" is important? She must consider me a nonentity, yet I can't get her out of my mind. Remember her! I can't forget her! She is real.

She was born in Manchester, England. But, is she friend or foe? I met Celia on board the ship Queen Elizabeth II in the middle of the Atlantic Ocean. Even there, she disappeared. Four weeks later, on Riverside Drive in New York City, Celia again surfaced in my life. She asked for a dance and we moved to Peggy Lee's album, "Fever." We shared a passionate kiss—my first kiss. But, she disappeared. Two years later, in Los Angeles, through my good friends Carol and Elaine, Celia was once more incarnated. Once again, too briefly with me and she was gone. But when I saw her in my dreams, when she stopped me from entering through the big gate as I felt myself drowning in the pool, she was pregnant. In my subconscious state of mind, she is carrying a baby and I know the child is mine.

CHAPTER VIII

I Love My Child. My Child is Home.

The message was now clear to me that it was not just an issue of Celia. It was not about Kayleen or the music angel. The biggest mystery yet to unfold was yet to be born. Somewhere between the spirits of these three lady figures, was a real child, my baby. I knew it couldn't be by the music woman, she forbade physical contact beyond placing my hand on her breast. With Kayleen, intimacy was created. With her, the sex was brief, intermittent, almost staged. No, with the measure of substance required for parental selection, it had to be Celia, but I felt there was a mystical conspiracy to keep me in the dark.

The time had come for me to connect with my real home. I returned to Africa. When my feet hit the soil, my blood began to flow again. I felt alive and aware of myself for the first time in many years. I was greeted, as is the custom, by most of my family. My parents were especially happy to see me, although I could tell immediately that they were expecting more than just me to arrive. "Where is Celia and your daughter," she whispered through tears of joy as we embraced.

I was shocked to hear the name Celia from my mother. In England, Cecilia is abbreviated as Celia. In Africa, Sesilia becomes Selia. How did my parents hear of this name? It was perplexing but I refused to deny myself this fantasy. I simply replied, my wife and my daughter were very well but they are not here with me. They will join me later and you will have a chance to see them.

My answer seemed to assuage everyone for the moment. Still, I wondered where the information came from. Never had I spoken about Celia with anyone in my family.

However, in anticipation of my "family's" arrival, my cousin Jibade had prepared very comfortable accommodations for us in his apartment. He had planned to give us the royal treatment in his apartment about two miles from Lagos Island. A beautifully adorned king sized bed was the focal point of the large master suite. It was draped by a white knitted mosquito net designed to keep us comfortable and safe from the insects. What a tribute he planned to welcome my wife and daughter to the family. Unfortunately, it was only I who arrived to enjoy these warm gestures from my kin. I slept alone.

On my first night back in my homeland I fell into a deep sleep. Again, I traveled into a strange and sweet dream. I dreamed of the arrival of Celia and her beautiful daughter. Her daughter was about nine years old with coffee brown skin and dark eyes. She was the most stunning black and white child I had ever seen. She was slim but not thin. Her shoulders were high, just like Celia's, but her feet and nose were mine. This little girl was adorable and I was very happy that we were a family at last.

In this dream state, I flashed back to the voyage on Queen Elizabeth II from Southampton to New York. Only this time, in my mind, the three of us walked the same road that I truly had taken with Celia. Upon arriving in New York City, Celia took our daughter and traveled to Los Angeles, California. Four weeks later, Celia returned to New York to look for me. By this time, we were out of touch. Through her power of intuition, she was able to track me down to a party on Riverside Drive. We were together for only fifteen minutes. We had a passionate kiss. The dream moved quickly forward to the engagement dinner at Elaine's home. Quite suddenly, the journey ended. I don't know what interrupted this travel to a place I preferred to my reality, but some indescribable force awakened me. Again, I found myself alone in a large bed. The netting above me seemed to entrap me in the physical realm. I shed a silent tear as I gazed upward and lamented my consciousness. The dream could have been truth. The wonderful child I walked with through my mind was mine and I loved her.

CHAPTER IX

Super Natural Belief—YORUBA MYTHOLOGY

The Yoruba Nation or Yoruba race occupies Southwest of Nigeria, including Porto Novo, Benin Republic in West Africa. Before the introduction of Christianity and Islam, the Yorubas were very religious people who believed in only one God. The Almighty, the Creator of Heaven and Earth, is known in Yoruba language as Olodumare.

However, Yoruba also have several divine gods as intermediaries between them and Olodumare (God). I was born to a Yoruba family in Oyo Town, the Seat of old Oyo Empire. Although most Yorubas accepted Christianity and Islam, occasionally, when there is a need for a quick answer to a problem or problems, some Yorubas still consult with traditional power.

Some of the most powerful Yoruba Gods are "Sango," the God of thunder accompanied with lighting as a weapon to destroy his enemies. Sango is a fearful Aalfin, the former king of the Old Oyo Empire (who lived long ago). He has raised himself above all men, he became superman and his followers accepted him as their God. Sango's first wife, "Oya", the Goddess of the River, is widely believed to be descended from River Niger.

"Iyemaja", the Goddess of the Sea. She was kind and gentle. She had the power to help women who were barren. She helped them produce many offspring.

"Ori," One's Head. This is a divine God. Ori is a custodian of wisdom and destiny.

"Ifa", Orumila Oracle is a divine prophet. Ifa is God of Wisdom, a teacher and savior. He's a spiritual being. He descended from heaven and landed on earth. He exemplified hope, love and peace. Ifa, according to Yorbuas, is the art of cleanliness. He is regarded as a source of wise counsel and prophetic measures. Ifa-Oracle works with "Ori" and is the only Yoruba God that has access to Olorun, the God in Heaven. Only "Ifa" knows the secret of human beings. "Ifa" is the only God empowered with extra wisdom. The Yorubas believe that he knows the secrets of human existence. Many Yorubas still consult with "Ifa" in every serious matter concerning their families. He can predict the future and reconnect you to the past occurrences.

For fourteen years of my traveling around the world, I did not communicate with my parents. They did not know if I was alive or dead. The uncertainty and fear prompted my parents to consult with "Ifa" oracle.

CHAPTER IX

Return to Africa

When my mother died, my life was very empty. I felt as though I was being swallowed by depression. I had no one close to me. I could not make my "wife and child" materialize from my dream. I was alone in the world. I traveled to my homeland for the funeral but I did not go to our family home. I decided to stay in a hotel and be totally alone in my loneliness. After some hours of sustained mourning, I forced myself to venture outside into the sunlight. It really was a perfect day when I permitted myself to enjoy it. The sky was very blue and the sun shone radiantly upon the clean, urban ambience. After walking around pretty aimlessly for what seemed like hours, I once again felt the need for my solitude. As I was walking back to the room, there was no person present around me. The corridors seemed abandoned. Within seconds after I closed the door to my room, I heard a soft knock.

To my amazement, I opened the door to find an absolutely gorgeous ebony lady in front of me. She was a stunning female specimen, yet there was a supernatural aura about her. We exchanged no words, only gazed into each others' eyes. After nearly a minute, she gracefully turned and walked away from me.

"Hello, may I help you?" I called to her, but she had vanished.

It was time for my mother's funeral and I tried to prepare myself for this farewell tribute. I showered and donned a traditional outfit for the service. This time, when I opened the door to exit, a note was attached to it. The note read: "My name is Selia and you will see more of me."

Two weeks later, I was traveling in the university town of Zaria located in the northern part of the country. It was a very hot Saturday afternoon with temperatures reaching above 100 degrees. With nothing else to do, I jumped into my car and started driving toward the center of town. While I was stopped at an intersection, I glanced in my rear view mirror and I noticed a very striking lady. Her skin was smooth and brown and she had long light brown hair that seemed to blend with her complexion. She was dressed in white lace with white slippers and she was approaching my vehicle.

I watched her walk to the passenger side of the car and open the door. I might have felt that I was being carjacked if I wasn't so intrigued with her beauty. She sat next to me and I fell in love at first sight. Her beauty was overwhelming but her mannerisms were subdued. All I knew at the time was that I must have her, all other issues notwithstanding.

She looked straight into my eyes and commanded me to drive her to a building that resembled a church. I was instructed to wait in the car as she disappeared for about fifteen minutes. Upon her return, I was again instructed to drive to another location. This time, she took me to a wooded area, which was the location of a government reservation area (GRA). All GRA's in Nigeria are designed for British colonial officers and, therefore, they are normally very attractive tracts of land.

By now, it was clear who was totally in charge of this little game we were playing. She was winning it and in doing so, she was winning my heart. She disembarked from the vehicle and looked at her watch. It was about two o'clock. She turned to me and dismissed me but not without ordering me to return at four o'clock. I drove off and went home for a nap. I was fatigued yet fearful of missing my deadline. Restlessly, I awaited my next mission.

As instructed, I returned to the place at four. At first, she was nowhere in sight, but suddenly appeared next to my side of the car. She instructed me to drive away from her slowly, but to keep my eyes focused on the rear view mirror. I would be getting a sign from her when she wanted me to stop the car. I watched her, and she never moved from the spot. When directed by her, I stopped the car and she again walked toward it. Once more, she entered the vehicle and sat very close to me.

"Where do you live?" she inquired.

"I live very close," I answered, not really expecting her next response.

"Let's go to your house."

When we arrived at my home, I offered her food and drink in a perfunctory manner but she was not interested. Her eyes directed me to the bedroom. I acquiesced and soon we were engaged in a very passionate kiss. Suddenly, my thoughts were transferred back to Riverside Drive in New York City where I first kissed Celia. But here, in my own bedroom, with this angel, the experience was becoming even more intense.

Wildly, lasciviously, lusciously, we made love for two hours. The sensations were heightened but strangely, I never ejaculated. I never wanted the session to end, but, of course, it had to. The African sun began sinking into the west and the temperature was cooling down. She arose from our bed and walked to the window as if entranced. Her silhouette was the most gorgeous thing I had ever seen. Her long slender body was fully exposed and traced by her silky tresses. I was in love.

I wished and prayed that this human angel would stay with me forever. I hoped that she would give me a daughter, a replica of her likeness. Yet, our lovemaking did not yield the seeds required for her garden. As I was looking at her, lost in thought, she turned to me and requested that I take her one more place. I told her that I would take her anywhere she wished but I wanted to be with her. I wanted us to be together forever. I asked her to marry me and she said, "You are my love I shall always be a part of your life, but we must go now."

I drove her across town to a construction site. She took me inside the partially completed building where another lady emerged. They personally exchanged greetings. The evening was beginning to cloak the day and light precluded me from seeing the other woman. I moved closer to the pair and my angel spoke to me.

"Layi, I would like you to meet Kayleen."

"How could this be?" I was shocked and terrified. The mention of the name of this woman who tried to replace Celia in my heart made me mentally confused. My angel turned again to me and said, "I am traveling to the City of Jos tomorrow. I will be back to Zaria on Wednesday at five o'clock. Please meet me here."

"Of course I will," I obediently replied. "Before you leave, please tell me your name." "My name is Celia, Celia Parsons."

With that, Celia disappeared into the night with the woman she called Kayleen. At precisely five o'clock on Wednesday, I returned to the location as instructed. Only this time, a huge burly man emerged from the building. When he asked me what I was doing there, I told him that I was supposed to meet Celia.

"You are looking for whom?" he gruffly asked me. "This building is off limits to the public. I am the security guard and these premises are private. No one is allowed to be here but the construction crew. I have never heard of anyone named Celia and she certainly isn't here. Now, I would advise you to leave."

Like the broken man that I was, I limped back to my car and sat speechless. I waited there for what seemed like hours hoping to get a glimpse of my lady. I affixed my gaze into the rearview mirror. She was gone—vanished from my life.

One week later, I boarded Nigerian Airways for the one-hour flight from Kaduna to Lagos. The plane landed at six o'clock in the evening and I immediately grabbed a taxi to Victoria Island where I planned to stay with friends for a few days. Victoria Island is eight miles from Lagos Airport. About halfway to Victoria Island, at Eko Bridge overpass, there was a traffic bottleneck. Cars were literally at a standstill. Sitting amidst the honking and exhaust fumes, I relived the recent moments with Celia over and over in my mind. Even as I flew away from the place of our rendezvous, I was still confident that she would truly be as she had spoken, always a part of my life.

Suddenly, the opening of my taxi door surprised me. The experience was surreal as I laid my eyes on a woman who looked exactly like Celia. I said, "Excuse me, this taxi is taken."

She returned a smile and spoke, "I know it is taken, by us—you and me."

Again, I was drawn into the game. "Where are you going?"

She smiled again and replied, "I am going wherever you are going. Yes, I am going to Victoria Island."

Traffic began to move again and the driver took us to my destination. When we arrived at the house, five of my friends were waiting for me for a quiet dinner. No one appeared surprised by the presence of this mysterious woman. She seemed happy to be in the company of my friends, and I wanted to introduce her. I did not know who she was but she was with me. As if she could read my mind, she took it upon herself to make introductions. "Hello fellows, my name is Celia. I met Layi on the plane. He is my very good friend."

She and I had never exchanged names. After dinner, we played a game of Monopoly. Celia was very skillful. I was getting tired, and my friends showed us to our room. Celia and I spent the night together. A blissful, passionate night with this woman made me certain that she was destined to be mine. If only I knew how to capture her.

In the morning, I asked her if she wanted to stay with me longer. She asked me to call a taxi for her but promised to meet me for lunch at the very exclusive Eko Meridian Restaurant. As was her pattern, she did not show up for our date. As I sat alone in the café sipping a glass of wine, I felt a strange calm. I saw flashes of her beautiful countenance and remembered the words she spoke in Zaria. "I shall always be a part of your life." I knew I would see her again.

CHAPTER XI

In the United Kingdom

I was fortunate to have been one of the people sponsored by the British Council to study cooperative education at the Co-Operative College Stamford Hall, Loughborough, England. This program is affiliated with Loughborough Institute of Technology and is unquestionably one of the finest British educational institutions. The programs were scheduled to be completed in nine months, and there were more than ten participating countries from the Commonwealth of Nations. This included participants from Africa, Asia, the West Indies, and the South Pacific. This cultural and intellectual melting pot offered enormous opportunities to glean information about previously unknown people and places in the world.

The program began with an organization of student government. I was elected to the office of Secretary of Finance. My peers nicknamed me, “Chancellor of Exchequer.” During college, I had become a model of mediocrity. I was never particularly committed to academia but I considered myself a superior candidate to most of the other competing students. I was relieved to find most of the lecturers in the program very enlightening, with the exception of John Lauder. He believed in “divide and conquer” and usually favored students from certain countries. In addition, he was a drunk.

Despite his shortcomings, John was instrumental in my selection to work with the British Ministry of Education for one full year after the completion of the program. My special project involved troubled youth in Manchester, which naturally necessitated traveling to this city. In my life, travel always seemed to beget another Celia saga.

I worked in Manchester City regularly. It constituted about a two-hour drive from Loughborough to the cooperative headquarters. One evening as I arrived at the train station in Manchester ahead of the scheduled departure, I walked to the magazine stand to select some reading material for the ride home. After paying for my book, I accidentally bumped into a lady standing very close behind me. I turned to apologize and was momentarily speechless. The face starting back at me was so familiar.

"I'm sorry. Please excuse me," I said.

"It's okay, I should not have been standing so close to you. Where are you traveling to this afternoon?

"I am going to Nottingham."

"I am going to Loughborough via Nottingham. My name is Layi. And you? "What is your name?

"My name is Celia."

"Do we have time for a cup of tea before the train departs?"

Celia and I walked to the restaurant and ended up having a nice dinner. I felt she was strangely familiar. We boarded the train and sat side-by-side for three to four hours. I was inside her aura. It was love again. We shared small conversation. She told me that she was born and raised in Manchester. I told her that I had traveled extensively inside the United Kingdom, on the Continent and in the United States.

"I have been to New York City, Chicago, Los Angeles and Honolulu," she shared.

"Celia and I have been to every city you mentioned," I volunteered. "I was in New York for fourteen months. I then moved to Los Angeles where I stayed for four years. En route to L.A., I stopped in Chicago. From Los Angeles, I moved to Honolulu. I attended the University of Hawaii and lived on the island of Oahu for six years."

"Where is home Layi?"

"I am originally from Nigeria. I am very sure you know much about Nigeria. Your country, Great Britain, colonized Nigeria for over fifty years and that made Nigerians Commonwealth Citizens."

"Would you like to hold me for colonization Layi?"

What an off the wall question I thought. "No, not at all Celia. I just want to keep you with me forever, in sickness and in health and for richer or poorer. I guess though, I may need to request permission from the Queen." I couldn't believe the words were pouring from my mouth.

"I'm sure Her Majesty will grant your request Layi." This woman was not only beautiful and intelligent; she had the most valuable characteristic of all, a sense of humor. The train ride was going too fast. When we arrived in Nottingham, I gave my address and telephone number to Celia. Although I waited patiently, there was no further communication from her.

Four weeks passed and I was on a chartered bus tour to Oxford University with students from the co-op program. Oxford is a remarkable campus, with facilities spread all over the city. It reminded me of Yale University in New Haven, Connecticut, with the impressive historical architecture, spires and inherent dignity. I was humbled by the very soil under my feet on this remarkable campus.

I strolled aimlessly for what seemed like hours and found myself in the University library. When I entered through the magnificent arches, the first sight that caught my focus was none other than Celia. She saw me too and smiled knowingly. I don't know who moved more quickly to embrace, but in a matter of seconds, we were embracing. She said that she had been waiting for me.

We decided to find a quiet restaurant to lunch and visit. The waitress gave us a table for two overlooking the College of Agricultural Economics. My thoughts flashed back to Honolulu and I told Celia that I attended a college of agricultural marketing. This opened an opportunity for me to inquire more of my angel. I knew so little about her and yet nothing more needed to be known.

Celia told me of her aspirations to become an actress. Shakespeare was her special interest but she confided that she was auditioning for a part in "Gulliver's Travels," the movie slated to star Ted Danson. She also told me that she had a twelve-year-old daughter who would be following in her passion for the theater. Celia had never been married.

I was with Celia for nearly two hours and wished the time would never end. When our interlude was over, I asked how I could get in touch with her. I had no address, no phone number and very little background. She said, "I don't write letters or make phone calls, but when I am ready to see you, anywhere in the world, you will see me. I shall always be a part of your life."

She looked at me very sympathetically and continued, "Believe it or not, I will see you in a few days." I put my hands on her shoulders and gave her a passionate kiss. She was consuming me. We parted with this, my gesture of deep love and anticipation.

I returned to Loughborough and life continued as usual. I did not expect to hear from Celia. She had made it totally clear who was in control of our rendezvous. Four weeks later, it was time to go on a one week holiday in London. I traveled with my customary tour group and we stayed in dormitories at the London School of economics. Our accommodations were comfortable, the city was breathtaking, but I was bored. I decided to take a bus to York.

I don't know why I was drawn to York. Few destinations in England have such rich history and natural beauty. Thirteenth century walls encircle the city, approximately three miles in diameter within the city gates. I walked the footpath of the medieval walls, determined to absorb the vibrations of the entire enclave. I walked to the museums and experienced the Norman, Medieval, Saxon, Georgian and Victorian flavors of York. I wandered the city until I became fatigued and returned to my hotel for rest.

Upon waking on my second day in this place, I embarked upon a trip to the National Railway, Britain's largest single body of historical railway materials. The collection covers all aspects of railway history, from locomotives to uniform buttons worn by the Pullman porters.

There was also a collection of royal coaches from Queen Victoria's reign to King George VI, and beyond. I missed no section of the museum for it was quite educational and interesting.

I began to feel Celia and found myself always looking for her face in each crevice and crowd in the city. My funds were beginning to run pretty low and I needed to make crucial decisions about joining my group in London. The next stop on our itinerary was Abersywyth, Wales. I didn't want to miss the connection.

Abersywyth is one of the small coastal towns in Wales, located along the Atlantic Ocean. The Welsh people are very friendly and hospitable. Again, I toured the city in awe of one of Great Britain's as well as the world's best libraries. The best sight of all was an old abandoned castle overlooking the sea.

The stately ancient structure welcomes thousands of visitors every month. Today I was one of them and, ironically, so was Celia. I spotted her shortly after I entered the gates. She was strolling with a man and appeared not to notice me. I followed the duo into the bowels of the castle where he began to photograph Celia. Although the background was cold, stone and dank, Celia was hot. She raised her head, lifted her beautiful and dimensional eyes to meet mine and said, "Nice glasses."

I was dumbstruck. She was referring to a pair of new eyeglasses that I had purchased before left London. Without another word, she walked away from me and disappeared into the cavernous domain. I could speak nothing further. I watched her go and felt the emptiness and sadness that defined the lower level of this castle. What other atrocities must be recorded in these frigid walls.

Ascending back up into daylight, I found my group in search of me. It was time to continue our journey to the University of Sterling in Scotland. It was time for me to continue again with only a whetted appetite for Celia. Shortly after our arrival in Scotland, the group leader summoned us for a meeting to discuss the next day's itinerary. I was unable to focus on the discussion at hand. I became overwhelmingly fatigued. I was so depressed that I easily succumbed to sleep that evening. I surrendered to my dream state.

Experts have written that dreams are, "strange, mysterious phenomena that spontaneously happen on the night shift of life." But is there some deeper meaning behind this universal experience? The dreams are certainly a valued commodity throughout the recorded history of humankind. So, this night could be documented in the annals of this enigmatic state.

My slumber deepened and I could sense a descent into another realm of existences. Here, none other than Celia greeted me. Her slim body, milky smooth skin, blue eyes and silky long black hair all appeared before me with absolute clarity. Instantaneously, we were somehow transported to a beautiful park with many trees, flowers and foliage. One tree in particular stood out among the other arboreal guardians. As with Biblical precision, this tree alone bore fruit. I could smell the fragrance of the fruit but it seemed too high above me to reach. I knew somehow that it was forbidden. Celia walked underneath the tree, lifted her arms and two pieces feel into her grasp. She placed the fruit in the basket, took my hand and led me to another area.

This part was not in Europe. We were far away from anything I had recently experienced during my journey. The scents of spices and herbs made me think of India. We were now in another garden with trickling waterfalls and statues carved from precious gems. Celia led me to a large carpet in the center of the garden and bade me to sit down.

"Do you have any wishes to be fulfilled Layi?" she spoke reverently.

"Yes," I replied to her as I simultaneously dropped to my knees.

"Celia, will you marry me? I wish to marry you here, here, in this moment."

"Very well," she said. "I will marry you as we stand on this beautiful carpet, but I want the ceremony performed by an Indian Christian priest." she continued, "I have summoned him and he will be arriving soon in a small boat. He is bringing our wedding dresses with him."

No sooner than the words were spoken, I saw a small boat appear on the water. A holy man emerged from it carrying a white silk sari and gold jewelry that he handed to Celia. He turned to me and presented a blue silk wedding garment.

Transformed, we stood before him. Only the three of us were present. Soft breezes wafted the smell of jasmine and ginger, birds sang and the melody of water cascading over rock provided music for our vows. Blue skies and shimmering sum gave life to the rose blossoms which seemed to extend their leaves to embrace our love. I tasted the sweetness of her mouth as Celia pressed her body closer and closer to mine. All senses were invoked to conjure the magic of this moment. My bride clenched me tightly as we boarded the boat and floated down the narrow river through the garden splendor. The narrow river soon gave way to the wider mouth of the River Clyde in Scotland. Just as I gleefully marveled at our miraculous return to Scotland, I was jolted by the screeching noise of an alarm clock. It was four o'clock, but I was not ready to surrender the dream.

I opened my eyes, but she was gone. I arose and started my morning bathing ritual. The warm water made me relaxed and I decided to try to fall asleep once more. This time, as I drifted, I was swept into a movie of memories. I relived the initial meeting with Celia on the QE II. I heard the sound of "Fever" playing in the background as we danced in New York City. I returned to Elaine's party in the University of Hawaii. I was walking a long, lonesome path so familiar to me in my conscious state. All at once, I saw her. Celia was once again standing before me, beckoning me to join her at a cottage in the forest. It was time to continue our honeymoon. She looked very desirable and I was so thankful to have found her again.

Our honeymoon suite was 300 square feet. A king-sized bed with a solid gold frame was the centerpiece of the room. The mattress and pillows were crafted in velvet and the bedspread was pure white Indian silk. The ambience was enchanting. As if the scene had been choreographed, we moved toward the bed never losing the gaze between us. Gently, I lifted her to the bed and lowered my body onto hers. The flames of our love ignited us both. I drew even closer to her and pressed my chest into her breast. She opened her lips slightly and my tongue found its way. I imagined that the flavor of our lust could not be rivaled by the taste of the forbidden fruit I have coveted before. She was erotic and sensual and I knew by her signals that she was also a virgin. This only fueled my passion while making me even more blessed to be presented with this special gift. I wanted to be gentle and I wanted to give her pleasure beyond any primal expectations.

Our love dance lasted for hours and our mutual pleasure lingered beyond the suite. I had never been happier. For the very first time, I knew instinctively that I was finally in control of Celia. I had given her what she wanted and needed and the look of calm and contentment I sensed from her body and saw on her face gave me no further reason for insecurity. Beside her, inside her, we both drifted to sleep.

Perhaps it was the absurd dichotomy of sleeping during a dream that brought me back into a waking state, but as fate would dictate, I was disturbed by the voice of someone calling my name. Dazed, confused and reluctant, I opened my eyes only to find the tour guide calling the group to breakfast.

"What? I had already been nourished from the chalice of a goddess. How could anything less be satisfying?"

The morning journey was to Sterling Castle, which housed many of the Stuart Kings and Queens of Scotland. The castle had strategic importance because it was the gathering place of many of Scotland's historical giants. Wallace, Bruce, Mary Queen of Scots, John Knox and Charles Edward Stuart all spent hours within the walls of this impressive structure. Upon leaving, we moved our party to Glasgow and enjoyed a reception with the Lord Mayor of Glasgow. This festivity was followed by a stop at a Scotch Whiskey refinery and finally to the mouth of the River Clyde. Briefly, I escaped to the sanctuary of my private thoughts. I reminisced about the hours before when I shared this view with my Celia, my fleeting bride. The rest of the day was long and tedious. I longed for a bed in order to return to my dream state. At the end of the day, when I could finally close my eyes, Celia was nowhere to be found. The next morning, however, I awoke to find a small bouquet of Bird of Paradise next to my bed with a note that said, "I hope to see you in South America. Celia P."

CHAPTER XII
Extra Sensory Perception

Since childhood, I always knew that I was gifted with powers beyond the norm. I have been able to perceive events before they occur and have subconsciously communicated with the dead. My beloved mother, who passed away nearly two decades ago, comes to me frequently from beyond to discuss important family business. I have always tried to be cognizant of and respectful of the messengers, whether seen or unseen. Being aware of these powers, the seeds of which we all possess, is the first step in unlocking them. It is my goal to diligently strive to become more acute at developing my physic acumen.

Celia is far advanced in this realm. Although I believed that she would see me in South America, when I received the Bird of Paradise bouquet from her, I had no plan to travel to this part of the world.

It was late autumn and I needed cataract surgery on my eyes. Vision on a physical level had always been a challenge for me. Without my glasses, I am nearly blind. The eye surgery was successfully performed at Queens Medical Center. A friend drove me home and upon arrival, I was very pleased to discover a letter from my good friend, Carlos, a college friend from Brazil. I had not been in communication with him for nearly eight years. His letter indicated that he had returned to his native county to live and would very much like to renew our friendship. He invited me to come to South America for a holiday.

Less than one month later, I was on Varig Airlines, en route to Rio de Janeiro. Carlos lived in Brasilia, the capital city of Brazil. For no particular reason, my reservation was not made directly to Brasilia, but rather routed me through Rio. The seven-hour overnight flight from Lagos was very smooth.

On arrival, the customs and immigration procedures were meticulous and thorough. After retrieving my luggage, I walked out of the airport to get a taxi. But to where? I had no hotel reservation and knew no person in Rio to advise me. Quite frankly, it was not my original plan to stop over in this spectacular city. I really didn't know why I was here. As I stood daydreaming at the taxi depot, a Volkswagen Taxi stopped right where I was standing. The driver opened the door and invited me to enter. To my pleasure and amazement, the driver was a young and very tantalizing woman. She was svelte and brown, with lighter brown hair and her personality reminded me instantly of Celia. Without hesitation, I quickly entered her domain and waited for her to carry me to the adventure that I was there to experience.

Hotel Rio Copa is very close to the center of all attractions. It is about two hundred meters from the beach of Copacabana and a ten minute drive to downtown. Conversation in the taxi was pretty innocuous and I was beginning to feel the affects of jet lag. The striking beauty of my chauffeur kept me fairly awake and attentive. When we arrived at our destination, Celia escorted me inside and made certain that check-in went smoothly. I offered her money for my ride but she adamantly refused as though I had offended a vintage friend.

"Get some rest and I will meet you for breakfast tomorrow morning." With those parting words, she exited the hotel and I only hoped that she had not exited my life. Nevertheless, I heeded her advice and slept for about twelve hours. As promised, the phone rang early the next morning and Celia instructed me to meet her in the lobby in thirty minute.

At this point, I started trying to reconstruct the events since my arrival as I showered and headed for the lobby. There was no drum roll or announcement, but when Celia walked through the doors of the hotel, it was as if everyone had been notified. All heads turned and I was beaming with pride as she approached me and planted a warm and very wet kiss on my lips.

This time, Celia was driving a new red Puma. She nicknamed her hot Brazilian sports car, "Little Red Rooster." She drove so aggressively that I found myself gripping the door handle in angst. Were it not for the fact that I knew in my higher sense that she was my guardian angel, I would have been petrified by the ride she was giving me.

"How fortunate I was to meet you Celia. How could you know that I was in need of a friend in Rio? I tried some levity.

"Don't be silly, I know everything," she mused. "I knew that you were coming to South America and I made your hotel reservation for you. You only have a short holiday. Rio de Janeiro is quite a magnificent city and I want to share it with you."

The tour began at Corcovado, the Statute of Christ. This is the landmark that identified Rio de Janeiro. The statue stands 2,330 feet above sea level and watches over the city. For visitors, it provides a panoramic view of both sea and mountain. It is a breathtaking, world famous vista. Our next stop was Aguca, aka Sugarloaf, near Guanabara Bay. There, we rode the cable car to the top of the rock and then to Arcos da Lapa. Santa Terez Lapa arches Santa Tereza. Located in the Largo da Lapa's quake, in the structure, it contains forty-two arches in two tiers.

Stopping only briefly for respite and refreshments, our whirlwind journey through the city led us next to Paradise of the Planet and trees from the four corners of the earth. Jardim Botanico offers some of the most lush and gorgeous gardens to be found on the planet. Finally, on to Copacabana, the widest beach in Rio and home of beach soccer, volleyball and beautiful people. Curving lazily along the Atlantic, the beach stretches for about four kilometers.

This beach is famous for love, lust and romantic encounters. That day, Celia and I were to hold true to the legends of the land. Here, we stopped in one of the most isolated areas on the shore and sat quietly buried in each other's soul. After the sun was completely surrendered to the horizon, I surrendered my love to Celia's guardianship. We stretched our bodies side-by-side and gazed into the night sky for hours. Only the stars would witness the passion between us.

As I drifted to sleep with my arms still locked around Celia, I felt once again transported from Copacabana to a wide river in the east. I believe it was India. There was a colorful parade of ships and we were the guests of honor. There were people of all races and colors, white, black, red, brown and yellow represented in the parade. Their rainbow of hues was complemented by the array of roses, birds of paradise, palms, plumeria and violets. This was a wonderful place and anyone allowed to experience the magic was especially fortunate. There were no classes, diseases, devastation or disorder. All people were equally rich, healthy, loving and happy. This setting epitomized my ecstasy in this moment with my lady.

Celia and I spent the entire night on the beach. When awakened by the glow of the morning sun, without words, we boarded the "Little Red Rooster" and returned to my hotel. Reluctantly, I got out of the car. My anxiety was briefly leveled as Celia approached and engaged me in a long luscious kiss. She declined to go inside with me but promised I would see her again. I spent another three weeks in Brasilia alone.

CHAPTER XIII

Wings

From Rio de Janeiro, I returned to Los Angeles, lonely and heavy of heart. I was deeply in love with Celia and she was now my bride. Yes, it may have only been the stuff of dreams and fantasy but it was becoming more real in my life. God created us for each other and in spirit we were inseparable. Even sans physical contact, she always managed to find me wherever I went. She appeared in every city I visited, perhaps even guiding me to those destinations. I knew for certain that our connection would be eternal.

I awaited new communication from her in Los Angeles. I didn't know what form she might take this time, a beautiful white goddess or a flawless black African queen. As I waited, I decided to try touching base with my friends in Honolulu.

Nearly a week passed and I received a telephone call from Noel and Roseanne Francisco, former college roommates and great friends. They informed me of their plans to wed and invited me to serve as best man. I considered this a great honor and immediately returned to Hawaii. After the wedding, I began to feel more at home in Oahu. I decided to remain on the island and return to the University for a second degree.

Needing financial resources, I decided to take a job at the Holiday Inn, Windjammer Restaurant in Waikiki. My schedule was now very busy from 7:00 am to 11:00 pm. Still, I found time to think, wish and hope about Celia. One particular day, I walked down University Avenue to catch a bus to work. As the crowded bus pulled over to my stop, I noticed that the only seat available was next to a lady riding alone. It looked like the seat was reserved especially for me, so I gratefully sat down.

A second look at the lady swept me off my feet. I was overwhelmed and wanted to believe that this too was Celia incarnate. Everything about her physical characteristics was similar. She was extremely beautiful and appeared to be about 5'5" in height. She sported short light brown hair that framed her beautiful brown skinned face. She was wearing a short skirt that exposed beautiful legs which were a striking feature.

She appeared not to notice me as she read a novel. I was not to be ignored so I broke the ice.

"Hi. Are you from Hawaii? She appeared as though she could have been a native.

She raised her head and looked at me with beautiful glittering eyes. I knew it had to be my angel, Celia. "No, I am not from here. I am from the Midwest – Yellow Springs, Ohio," she replied.

"Are you a student at the University of Hawaii?"

"No, I am working at the Sheraton Waikiki."

"My name is Layi.

"That is a very nice name. My name is Sylvia. Nice to have met you Layi. This is my stop. Goodbye."

With those words, she got off the bus and left me wondering how to see her again. I returned to the same bus stop the next day but unfortunately she was not on the busy bus. I was strongly determined to find her. She left only one key piece of information but it was all I had. The Sheraton is a huge hotel but there cannot be too many people working there named Sylvia. I prayed that was her real name.

Luckily, I had many friends in Honolulu. One of them happened to work at the Sheraton. Her name was Michelle. I called her.

"Good afternoon Michelle. Today is your day off isn't it" I asked.

"Hi Layi! Yes, today I am off. I work at the Sheraton only on Thursdays and Fridays."

"Michelle, do you know somebody who works there named Sylvia?"

"Of course, she works with me. We actually met on the plane when we were traveling from Ohio to Hawaii. She is from the Midwest and so am I."

"You ladies from the Midwest are very beautiful. Can you give me Sylvia's number?"

Michelle gave me the phone number and I contrived a plan to see Sylvia again. I called the hotel to confirm her work schedule and invited my newly-wedded friends to accompany me for an evening at the Sheraton nightclub. Sylvia was employed as a cocktail waitress. Eager with anticipation, I arrived at the club around 10:00 p.m. I knew that she was scheduled to work until midnight. My heartthrob was nowhere in sight. But, I saw Michelle, who informed me that Sylvia was sent home early that evening because business was slow. We stayed for a while and listened to music but I decided it was time to take a more direct approach to Sylvia.

Simple research revealed her number listed in the phone book. I called and was pleased to find her friendly and cordial. I asked her if we could meet, but she was about to go to the mainland for a short holiday. She promised that we could be together upon her return. As she promised, we arranged a dinner for the following Friday night.

I arrived at her apartment in Manoa Valley. Trying to remember her features, I was amazingly pleased to find her as pretty as I had remembered. The night before our date, I dreamed of Celia and a little bird. Celia was obsessed with this little bird and gave it to me for safekeeping. When Sylvia opened the door, the first thing that came to my mind was the little bird I had dreamed of.

From that evening, she and I became good friends. We were inseparable and I was becoming as obsessed with her as Celia had been with the little bird. I was falling deeply in love with her—was it Celia? I kept transferring emotions, but Sylvia was treating me only as company. She had no reciprocal passion for me, although I knew she loved me deeply and cherished our relationship. Eleven months later, she returned to California. Another fleeting love ended.

I was in great pain and felt very alone. Unlike my typical separations with Celia, Sylvia and I remained in regular contact. She invited me to visit her in Sacramento. I was happy to see her again, but again, our relationship was platonic. The night before I left her, I experienced another uncanny dream. I was in an open field, the sky was very blue and clear. The field and sky merged in the distance. As I was standing in the field, the little bird I previously saw with mystic Celia, flew straight into my palm. I quickly embraced it and got some seed to feed it. I stroked it gently and wanted to nurture and give it tender love. I held the little bird and hoped it would stay with me forever.

Without any warning, the little bird suddenly flew away and disappeared in the blue sky. I left the next day for Honolulu. Again, sad and lonely, I was unable to forget my dream about the little bird. Once home, I resigned myself to focus on my future and disallow the torment of my emptiness. The next morning, a persistent tapping on my windowpane awakened me. It was as though it could not accept the fact that the glass separated us. I went outside and found the little bird lying below the window, quivering and weak. Its tiny wings were quiet. I picked up the small creature and tried to revive it. My heart wanted desperately to save it. I could feel the ceasing of movement in the palm of my hand. Just as calmly as the little bird had entered my life so the little bird had died.

CHAPTER XIV

Six Roses to a Shallow Mind

Traveling is, of course, my passion. I have traveled around the world by all means possible. When I was nine years old, I walked twenty-seven miles with my father to our family farm to help harvest crops. I have traveled on horseback, bicycle, caravan, canoe, car, Nigerian railway, British railway, Eurotrain, and many times I have crossed both the Atlantic and Pacific Oceans. I have fished the deep oceans off the coasts of Hawaii and journeyed to the thickest jungle in Africa for hunting. At the tender age of eight, I hunted rabbits, antelopes, deadly snakes, crocodile and lions with me and my family. We spent fourteen days in the jungle sleeping on its floor with only banana and palm leaves for comfort and protection. I was twice stung by scorpions and survived to tell this story. My father groomed me to be strong like a gladiator and my will is strong like iron. I acknowledge and honor both my conscious and subconscious mind. I know that both control and comprise who I am. Consciously, I attend to daytime activities and subconsciously, I surrender to my sleep state. Dreams working tirelessly during the nightshift of my life.

Joy, sorrow and concerns about employment, money and responsibilities define the conscious mind. To seek love and affection from friends and the opposite sex, experiencing the excitement and mysteries of the world. The desire to be a good citizen obeying the laws of the land, earning recognition and respect, these things I do consciously.

Subconsciously, however, I surrender to those powers beyond my obvious control. In this place, there are no worries, sorrow or disrespect. This is my perfect world and I have come to prefer living here. I am always around people of honor, people of all races and colors. It is the world that I believe God intended to create. STOPPED HERE This place, in my subconscious mind, is not tainted by prejudice nor polluted by human activities. There is no discrimination or racism. While the human factor evidences people of differing qualities, there are no inequities. Be they kings, queens or proletariats, there is abiding respect. I am a prince in my subconscious mind. I live in a mansion and I am highly revered. Celia is always on my path. But even in my subliminal existence, Celia eludes me. My love is steadfast, but Celia is elusive and I can neither capture nor escape her. Her power allows me to reincarnate her in various stages and places in my world. I am forced to relinquish myself to her as if she controls my very being.

I would prefer to view her as my guardian angel, when in fact, she is manifestly demonic. When Celia disappeared from my life, another woman very suddenly entered. She was slender and tall and had a beautiful face. Her skin was a mixture of black and white, actually more brown than anything else, and she was crowned by long, straight coal black hair. Her countenance resembled Asian tradition, but none of her physical traits mattered to me. What I always needed and desired was to enjoy the genuine and tender love of a woman and to be able to return an all encompassing love and passion. As Shakespeare wrote, "If music is the food of love, play on." I prepared myself for the theater of romantic euphoria.

In my subconscious mind, I mixed and dined with royalty. I shared conversations with Queen Elizabeth II and Prince Charles, Nelson Mandela, Robert and John Kennedy, and Gandhi. My world is always full and complete, except when my love is not at my side. During one exclusive dinner at the mansion in my dreams, I invited her to dine, but she failed to attend. Under a full and gentle moon, I decided to stroll alone in my garden. There were six beautiful roses along my path that seemed to be especially illuminated by the glow from above. As I strolled and admired the roses, I found myself at the doorstep of my love. I rang the bell and soon she appeared before me. In the background, I could hear Peggy Lee singing "Fever" ever so softly. Without a spoken word, I gazed into the eyes of my love. The depths of my emotion could not navigate her shallow mind. I silently extended the roses to her and with unbridled conviction, returned to my lonely mansion.

CHAPTER XV

Unsolved Mystery

Before the death of my little bird, love was meaningful and the nectar of life. After its death, love died too. My love life became scattered and upside down. There was something mystical about the little bird.

In 1969 when I met Celia and she gave me her telephone number, I was not very enthusiastic in calling her. Three days later, however, on a bright Sunday afternoon, a mysterious little bird flew through my window into my Los Angeles studio apartment. It landed on my dining room table where a piece of paper with Celia's telephone number was written. It seemed a coincidental reminder for me to call Celia, so I did. She sounded excited to hear from me as if she was actually awaiting the call. From that moment on our relationship was ignited and Celia always remained in complete control of us. She was the power and I was never even certain that she realized her capacity. Her magical power is her nature.

At the end of three months together, nothing seemed to change. Celia simply reincarnated herself into every other lady I met. In Los Angeles, she became Kayleen, Janet, Kett, Grace, and Sharon. In Britain, she reincarnated herself into Fiona and finally, in Africa, she because the beautiful Selia. Celia also escorted me around the world. We had our wedding in a beautiful Indian garden. I can never forget our train ride from Manchester City to
Nottingham, England. Our favorite meal was in the state-of-the art restaurant on the campus of Oxford University. Perhaps, the most significant stopover was the four-day romantic odyssey in Rio de Janeiro, Brazil. Where I am, consciously or subconsciously, Celia always seeks me out and transfers me to a mystical place.

Once when traveling to London from New York, I had another of my dreams. Celia came to the airport to meet me in the company of a twelve-year-old girl with brown skin and short brown hair. The pretty child looked interracial. The two special ladies had come to see me off. It was sweet but sad, as I was forced to bid farewell to my family. Yes, the scene was a family moment. Celia sent the little girl to give me a kiss goodbye. When sunshine chased my dream away, I knew somehow that this subconscious experience was very real. I was overwhelmed with a longing for this little girl. She was a part of me and I loved her. I loved her more that I ever loved myself.

When I arrived at Gatwick Airport in London, I took the British Railway to Victoria Station. From there, I rode the Tube, London's underground train, with the intent of reaching my hotel around Tottenham Court Road. The journey only involved two stops along the way before Oxford Circus station where I needed to transfer lines. At this point, I was struggling with an underground map and obviously appearing lost. Even in my frustration, I noticed a little girl approaching me.

"Excuse me sir, are you lost?"

With more than just a little amazement to see her, I replied,

"Yes, I am lost. I am trying to change to the Central line, for one stop to Tottenham Court Road."

"I thought so. Why don't you follow me?" The little girl took me to the correct train and actually boarded with me. At the end of our line, she took my hand and led me to the hotel. No further words were spoken until once inside. She turned to me, looked directly into my eyes and said "Goodbye sir. Have a nice day in London."

With this, the child vanished into the evening and I recognized immediately the similarity between her and the little girl with Celia. I felt instinctively that she was my daughter, my own flesh and blood. I exited the hotel desperately trying to identify her image among the crowd but she was gone. My blood ran cold, she was the same child and she did belong to me. I was determined to discover the truth.

After the seven-hour journey, I was fatigued and decided to rest. Early the next morning, I decided to begin my quest by tracing my steps to Oxford Circus. Once there, I walked from Regent Street to Piccadilly Circus. I walked back to Oxford Circus to Charring Cross Road and finally back to Tottenham Court. I checked every fast food restaurant and any other spot where kids might hang out. I found no clue to the little girl.

All of my life, I have wished to be married and to have children. The first one would be a baby girl. She would grow up to be a famous star or perhaps a professional tennis player. Although we were never married, my dreams revealed the true bond between Celia and myself. We parented a child. Finding her became the obsession of my life. All efforts appeared thwarted by the disappearance of Celia. How could I find my child when the mother had eluded me?

I decided to return to the United States and follow the path back to my most significant period with Celia. It was Los Angeles, California, February through May 1969. I also recalled my drowning experience in Hawaii and the vision of a pregnant Celia as I approached the tunnel of light. All of the information had been available to me, if only I could have processed it. Suddenly, I received a telephone call from a stranger. I was at work when a lady identifying herself as Devine Davis called and left a message on my voice mail.

"Hello, I got your name from one of your friends. I understand that you are searching for your daughter. I am also searching for my father. He is Nigerian and my mother is French. Here is my telephone number. Please call me and let us compare notes."

I was relieved and finally felt some optimism relative to my search. I wasted no time in calling the young woman. "Hello, Ms. Davis. This is Layi. I received a message from you regarding the search for your father."

"I am nineteen years old and have never met my father. He is from Nigeria. I was hoping you could help me. I understand you are searching for your daughter."

"Yes, although I am actually seeking her mother. If I can find her mother, I may also find my daughter. Perhaps we can help each other. I know a Davis family in Lagos. I will be going to Nigeria in one week. I will make some inquires and let you know what I am able to find. In the meantime, take good care. Goodbye for now Devine."

Five days later when I returned home from work, there was a message on my voice mail. "Hello Layi, I am happy to let you know that I have found my father. I will arrange for you to meet him sometime. Thank you for your friendship and support."

I was very happy for her and called her immediately to confirm the details. Devine was sure that an International Locator she had would assist me in my search for Celia Parsons. I decided to give it a try and contacted Mr. Klunder and Mr. Dunn, International Locators. They were very encouraging and promised to help me if I paid them $200 by credit card. I called my sister in New Jersey for assistance. After spending the two hundred dollars, I received about 750 pages of material and six cassettes with a letter which stated:

'While the subject of this package is adoption search, you will find that these same techniques can help you find almost anyone. To date, we have reunited thousands of families with the very same techniques and strategies that you will be learning shortly. In these 750 + pages of materials and six cassettes, we have covered virtually every scenario that you could possibly run into and many you probably won't."

Unfortunately, the information was useless to me and my money was wasted. I tried another avenue in U.S. Search. I explained my dilemma to this agency, which agreed to help me for a $100 fee to be paid only by credit card. Two weeks later, I received feedback from U.S. Search in the form of a very long letter:

Seeking Celia Parsons

Dear Layi:

Thank you for placing your order with U.S. Search. Please find enclosed the following results of your people search for Celia Parsons. U.S. Search has reunited more people than any other company. This is attributed to our vast resources, high success rate and our skilled counselors who offer the best customer service in order to guide you towards the best search strategy. Your search results contain names, and/or telephone numbers that corresponded with the information. You have been provided with U.S. listings without telephone numbers indicating an unpublished or unlisted number. We encourage you to contact listings without telephone numbers via the United States Postal Service.

From the information contained in these results, there is a high probability that you will locate Celia. This assumes, however, that Celia is not intentionally avoiding being found and that the information given is current and is currently in use. We look forward to your letter advising U.S. Search of your success.

Sincerely,
Andres Darkens

This letter was all that I received for the fee paid to U.S. Search. I made calls to all the telephone numbers provided, but most reflected numbers no longer in service. I wrote letters to all addresses given, but there was no response, save one. A wonderful lady from Lexington, Kentucky wrote:

Dear Layi:

I am sorry to tell you that I am not the Celia Parsons of your search. I am from Harlan, Kentucky, and I am 55 years of age. Good luck in searching for Celia.

Truly yours,
Celia Parsons

At this point, I decided to open direct communication with the YWCA in Los Angeles where Celia was staying when I first met her.

Dear Sir/Madam:

This is an unusual letter to receive but I am hoping you can help me. I am looking for a friend, Ms. Celia Parsons from Manchester, England. Celia was residing at your hotel in 1969.

Celia and I were good friends. However, I lost contact with her when I moved to the University of Hawaii. When I went back to the University on a visit, my friends informed me that a seventeen-year-old girl might be the result of our friendship. For the past ten years, I have spent a lot of time and money searching for Celia. Hopefully, if she can be found, the mystery of the 17-year-old girl can be solved. Unfortunately, I have not been successful. It has been too long and I am anxious to reconnect with my special friend,

Celia Parsons. Any help you offer will be greatly appreciated. I hope you will have some information about her in your records, such as her family's address in Manchester, England.

Please drop me a note in the self-addressed, stamped envelope enclosed. You are welcome to call me collect also. I am usually home from six o'clock in the evening, Eastern Standard Time.

I hope this letter finds you and your organization doing well.

Thank you

While I was awaiting a reply from the YWCA, there were more mysterious occurrences, probably designed to divert my attention away from Celia. The twelve-year-old girl who was with Celia in my dream at the airport in London suddenly appeared five years later. This time, she was seventeen and it was in the downtown district of Newark, New Jersey. I was alone at the bus stop when a biracial girl emerged. She was very petite and quite striking. She was dressed in a denim skirt outfit, adorned with a lot of beads around her neck. There was a single flower in her hair, Polynesian style. She was preparing to cross in front of me at Bradford Place when I noticed her as I waited at the bus stop.

Although our eyes never met, she intended for me to notice her. Bradford Place is a very narrow street, albeit busy with pedestrians and vehicle traffic. In the blink of an eye, she vanished. In one moment she was standing beside me and just as quickly she disappeared.

When my bus arrived, I was relieved to just get off that corner. Upon arriving home, I found a large brown envelope containing a round trip airline ticket from Newark to New Orleans. This was not a mystery. A family friend had invited me to spend time with them in the Crescent City and had sent me the tickets. I fell asleep with thoughts of Bradford Place and New Orleans.

My rest was not peaceful. I drifted into another slumber state and came upon this same mysterious young girl at the airport in New Orleans. In my dream, she arrived specifically to meet me and she looked exactly the way she did at Bradford Place, including the flower in her hair. She picked me up outside the airport, driving a red Italian sports car. The weather in New Orleans was cool and there was a gentle breeze. The city, as always, was electric. Music, aromas and culture filled the atmosphere.

We drove to the French Quarter, walked around Jackson Square and then on to the banks of the Mississippi. Here we boarded a luxurious Russian steamship and rode around the southern tip of the city. Afterward, we boarded a United States Navy ship and listened to live jazz and blues on the river. We went back to Bourbon Street and watched people milling about on foot and in horse and buggy. It may not have been Mardi Gras, but the flavor of this place is always festive. We were having a grand time together. Soon, she spoke to me in words that will forever be indelible on my heart. “Daddy, are you hungry?”

“Daddy.” I love the word Daddy. I was ecstatic to hear it. I had felt it for some time.

“Yes, my sweet, I am very hungry.”

We went to the very popular Court of Two Sisters on Royal Street and asked for seating. As we waited to be seated, I abruptly awakened from my dream and found myself still in my bed in New Jersey.

Three days later, when I actually arrived in New Orleans, I was not surprised to find the stage set exactly as I had dreamed, except my host arrived to greet me at the airport instead of my daughter.

My visit to the city was filled with the same parks, ships, restaurants and ambience of my dream. This was my first time in New Orleans but I amazed my host with my familiarity with the details of the area, especially the French Quarter. No sightings of my baby however. I returned home in about one week. In Newark, I found the following letter from the YWCA in my mailbox:

Dear Mr. Babatunde:

We received your letter of October 9 asking as to the whereabouts of your friend, Ms. Celia Parsons with whom you lost touch in 1969. Our sincere apology for not being able to help you in your search. Our records, unfortunately, do not go back to the 1960's. Additionally, the residential hotel where she resided was sold in 1990. We wish you our very best in your search to find Ms. Parsons.

And so, I encountered another disappointing turn of events in my quest for Celia Parsons and the even more hurtful absence of a relationship with my daughter. The mystery of her and our child will eventually be solved. In my heart, I know this is destiny. In the meantime, I will continue my life's journey around this world and others with love in my heart for the enigmatic mystic Celia.

The End

www.ingramcontent.com/pod-product-compliance
Ingram Content Group UK Ltd.
Pitfield, Milton Keynes, MK11 3LW, UK
UKHW020135250726
13967UKWH00002B/660

9 781425 124090